FOR
OTHERS

An aerial view of St. Joseph's Institution in 1962.

FOR
OTHERS

Editor

Alan Anand Johnson
St. Joseph's Institution, Singapore

World Scientific

NEW JERSEY · LONDON · SINGAPORE · BEIJING · SHANGHAI · HONG KONG · TAIPEI · CHENNAI · TOKYO

Published by

World Scientific Publishing Co. Pte. Ltd.

5 Toh Tuck Link, Singapore 596224

USA office: 27 Warren Street, Suite 401-402, Hackensack, NJ 07601

UK office: 57 Shelton Street, Covent Garden, London WC2H 9HE

National Library Board, Singapore Cataloguing in Publication Data
Name(s): Johnson, Alan Anand, 1976–   editor. | St Joseph's Institution.
Title: For others / editor, Alan Anand Johnson.
Description: Singapore : World Scientific Publishing Co. Pte Ltd., [2018]
Identifier(s): OCN 1004040032 | ISBN 978-981-3231-00-9 (paperback) |
    ISBN 978-981-3273-11-5 (hardback)
Subject(s): LCSH: St Joseph's Institution--Alumni and alumnae--Anecdotes.
Classification: DDC 373.5957--dc23

British Library Cataloguing-in-Publication Data
A catalogue record for this book is available from the British Library.

For any available supplementary material, please visit
http://www.worldscientific.com/worldscibooks/10.1142/10735#t=suppl

Desk Editor: Jiang Yulin
Designer: Jimmy Low

CONTENTS

———— ❧ ————

FOREWORD

St. Joseph's Institution is a very special school. Founded in 1852, it is the third oldest educational institution in Singapore and the first Catholic school in Singapore. Over her long and distinguished history, the school has contributed much to Singapore, not least by educating many boys who later went on to serve Singapore with distinction in a wide range of fields. While this in itself is worthy and substantial, what truly makes SJI special is the idea and ideal of service that is part of the essence of the school and her proud alumni. The school does not seek only to educate and nurture her students (which since 2013 has admitted girls to the IB Diploma programme) for success. This is only a means to an end and is reflected in the school's mission to empower her students "to become men and women for others". Ultimately, a Josephian who has been privileged to enjoy a Lasallian education is expected to live a life in service to others. Only then may she or he truly claim the mantle of being a "true Josephian".

It is therefore apt that this book is titled *For Others*. The selection committee has endeavoured not only to select distinguished alumni from different spheres, but also Josephians who embody the spirit of what it means to live a life "for others". Each of the men, and the one lady from the very brief time when SJI admitted girls to its pre-university classes, embody this trait of service to society and other people. The committee hopes that their lives and the examples of service that they embody will inspire students and alumni to lead lives consistent with the Lasallian core values of faith as the foundation, service as a way of life, while being part of a community that is supportive and nurturing.

On behalf of the school, I would like to acknowledge and thank the members of the selection committee, who are alumni of SJI:

Mr Anthony Lim	Dr Bernard Thio
Mr Derek Loh	Mr Jeffrey Low
Professor Leo Tan	Mr Mark Wong
Professor Michael Chia	Mr Roy Quek
Mr Tan Teck Hock	Mr Theodore Chan

who gave generously of their time to the preparation of *For Others*. They are all true Josephians worthy of the honour. I would also like to thank Reverend Fr Adrian for the generous support given by the school, Mr Alan Anand Johnson and Ms Eliza Lim for so ably supporting the committee in its work, all staff and students who in many large and little ways contributed to the publication of the book, and the publisher, World Scientific, and its helpful staff.

I hope you enjoy reading *For Others*.

Ora et Labora,
Professor Tan Cheng Han
(Class of 1980)

For

ART

Alvin Mark Yapp showing tennis superstar Li Na around The Intan.

ALVIN MARK YAPP

Founder of BusAds and The Intan,
Class of 1986

Alvin Mark Yapp honed his craft in service excellence at Singapore Airlines for nearly a decade before joining BusAds, a company his father had founded in 1983. BusAds quickly became the market leader in outdoor advertisement production literally moving from buses to the skies with aircraft decals.

Alvin is also the founder of The Intan, an award-winning Peranakan private home museum. Apart from introducing Peranakan culture to visitors and dignitaries, Alvin hosts art shows, charity concerts and plays music at The Intan. Some of the beneficiaries include the Singapore Children's Society and the Singapore Association of the Deaf. In 2009, Alvin was honored with JCI Top Outstanding Young Persons of Singapore Award and 2012 Singapore HR Leading CEO Award. Alvin is also the Ambassador for the Singapore Children's Society since 2014.

> *Alvin is also the founder of The Intan, an award-winning Peranakan private home museum.*

What was your experience as a Josephian and how has receiving an education in SJI impacted your life?

In many ways, I think SJI had an influence on who I am today. At that time it was a space to be who you wanted to be. I remember I had a PE teacher, who said that in SJI, we always produce the best; meaning that you are either the best scientist, the best doctor, the best cook, the best footballer, but whatever it is, we would produce the best in the fields that we are in. And I think SJI did! I mean I look back now and I look at the The Intan, my company, the work I do and I think that truly it was what the teacher said, that I am the best in my field. I may not be the President of Singapore, or a Nobel Prize winner, but in the space that I'm in, I choose to be a leader rather than a follower.

> 66
>
> *My Chinese used to be atrocious, and there was no way I could pass my Mandarin. But now today, I present Peranakan culture in Mandarin!*
>
> 99

My Chinese used to be atrocious, and there was no way I could pass my Mandarin. But now today, I present Peranakan culture in Mandarin! Half my workers are from China. I did interviews in Mandarin. I also did filming in Mandarin. So I think in SJI, it was a case when we were asked to do our best, but we were not condemned if we didn't meet basic expectations and that really was what pushed me and gave me the space to do what I wanted to do.

I was a terrible student. I would have copied and cheated, I would have had my parents come to school to bail me out, and I particularly didn't like studying at all. I found it boring, and I always found it was a challenge to try and cheat the teacher and the system. In my second year, I took the challenge to "spot" test questions; I studied the teacher's body language and the words he used in the class to predict what the test questions would be. That got me into the pure science stream in Sec 3. And being in the science stream in Sec 3 affirmed me that I had what it took to beat the school system in terms of spotting questions. I went on overdrive. I bought every colour highlighter I could find, and I practically highlighted every single question on every single textbook page. And lo and behold, I graduated and I qualified for a junior college, which of course was quite a shocker for my parents, as I was destined to be a *samseng*[1].

So one thing led to another and I went to NUS, and not only that I managed to get myself onto the honors roll, which of course was a big shock to everybody, and went into my dream job at Singapore Airlines as an Overseas Station Manager, where I could work and live in another country. And now I'm doing what I love to do. So I think SJI was a space where students can try their best to be academically clever or knowledgeable but it also was a space that had lot of comfort. I remember one Christian Brother. I don't know if he's still around. He was an Irish brother, a bit short. I think it was O'Brien is it? Anyway his accent was so difficult and I couldn't understand him at all. He was so old and from another generation. But what was so amazing was that every exam we went through, we were told that he would be in the chapel praying for peace for us,

Alvin says The Intan's vision is to inspire, just as SJI has.

---

[1]   Malay word for thug.

and that kind of story was what really made a whole lot of difference.

Do you think you've managed to live out Josephian values?

Yeah I think so, if you look at the website of the Intan, our vision is to inspire, and I think that's something that is very close to what SJI is doing: to inspire us to be best of who we are. When you walk into The Intan, we hope to inspire people to think about the impossible. I never grew up thinking that I would run and own a museum, but I did! And hopefully that allows people to push their passions.

The Intan is a private museum; 100% no funding from government. We have no paid staff: everyone is a volunteer. So SJI has taught me that firstly there is no such thing as a free meal. So we are successful,

Project Intan is a fundraising project that is close to Alvin's heart.

we make money, but at the same time, about half the time we give back to the community. We do plays, concerts and art exhibitions and that is service — kind of what SJI is about. It's not only to attend to the wealthy or to those who can afford, but it's those who have and have not, and that pushes us to be successful because we are different. I've got elderly visitors who cannot walk up the stairs, and we say "don't worry, we will bring down the things for you to see." These little gestures that we do, I believe it makes a difference.

The Intan was awarded National Heritage Board's inaugural Museum Roundtable Award for "Best Overall Experience" in 2011. It came with a trophy and a prize money of $5,000. I am honoured to be able to offer the prize money to SJI for their cultural programme, hoping it will inspire Singapore's next generation of leaders.

> *I've got elderly visitors who cannot walk up the stairs, and we say 'don't worry, we will bring down the things for you to see.'*

Fah Cheong says that Bro. McNally was his sifu.

CHONG FAH CHEONG

Sculptor and Cultural Medallion Winner, Class of 1961

I f you've taken a stroll down the Singapore River, then chances are you've seen this man's artwork.

Chong Fah Cheong is a 2014 Cultural Medallion recipient for his lifelong dedication to the practice of sculpture. The Cultural Medallion is presented to Singaporeans whose artistic excellence and contribution and commitment to the arts have enriched and helped shape Singapore's cultural landscape.

As a youth, Fah Cheong spent six years in SJI from Primary to Secondary 2 before following in the footsteps of his brothers to join the De La Salle Brothers' Novitiate in Penang and furthered his studies in Secondary 3 and 4 in St. Xavier's Institution. After completing his teacher's certificate in the following years, Fah Cheong decided to leave the religious life and return to Singapore to teach in St. Patrick's School.

Under the expert guidance of Brother Joseph McNally, Fah Cheong picked up the art of sculpting. Initially a self-taught skill, Fah Cheong's career as a sculptor began when Bro. McNally, then principal of the school, suggested that Fah Cheong make use

Romp in Penticton, BC, on Okanagan Lake by Chong Fah Cheong.

> **Bro. McNally is, in the Asian tradition, my Sifu.**

of fallen trees in the school campus to teach sculpting for his art classes. "Bro. McNally is, in the Asian tradition, my *Sifu*," says Fah Cheong as he recalls the personal encouragement and help he received from Bro. McNally. "His influence and encouragement and even his own work and how I used to see him working on his sculptures was very inspirational."

Despite living in Canada, Fah Cheong and his family are still Singaporeans. "I'm a true porcelain-green and Peranakan-Pink Singaporean," Fah Cheong says. His fondness of his childhood years spent in Singapore can be seen throughout all his works.

"Sculpting, to me, is how I view my experiences, my own childhood in Singapore, so I'm very quick to say that my works are my experiences of being myself."

EDMOND CHIN

―――――― ⚬ ――――――

Jeweler and Patron of the Arts,
Class of 1980

E dmond Chin is one of the foremost jewelers in
the world. His work has been lauded repeatedly
all over the globe. Several of his creations have gone
on to set world record prices at Christie's auctions.
For his contributions to the arts, he has been named
a Founding Patron of the Asian Civilisations
Museum. In 2013, he was selected to appear in the
book *21st Century Jewelry Designers* published by
the Antique Collectors' Club.

Edmond describes himself as a late bloomer. "I
was kinda like an underachiever I guess. I wasn't in
the top class. I was kinda just going through the
motions really. It took me a long time to figure out
where I was going and what I wanted to do. But
luckily I managed to get my act together towards the
second half of Secondary 3 and 4. It suddenly all
clicked and I got really good at studies mysteriously.
In the prelims I was in the top 10 at SJI; that was a
shock to all my teachers and to me as well. Very
strange."

At university, Edmond led an intriguing double life as a student and as a jewelry collector.

His exceptional results led him to the Oxbridge programme at Hwa Chong Institution and then on to Oxford University where he received his Master's in Geography. "I had by this time become very active in all sorts of extra-curricular activities; I was on the debating team, in the drama society, singing in church, doing theatre, lighting theatre, acting theatre and design theatre. I became very, very active in all sorts of other areas. And all this while, I was also studying the history of Indonesia — cultural anthropology, as expressed through jewelry."

This interest in jewelry led to an intriguing double life as a student and as a jewelry collector. "Now you ask, how can one person who's a university student afford to collect these things? I was quite enterprising in the sense that I had work; I did a lot of work. In university, I cooked. I used to host dinner parties for friends who wanted to eat Chinese food and they would pay me, and then I would go down to London and I would scout for interesting jewelry. I knew a couple who were jewelry collectors and I also knew one or two jewelers very well. I would go to London and I would offer to scout jewelry pieces for them for a percentage. They would pay me 10 percent for whatever they bought. So the first time round, they bought £30,000 worth of jewelry, they paid me £3,000, and I made money that way."

"I had been saving money and I had very strangely gotten this rather large collection of Southeast Asian jewelry. People had heard about my collection and I used to do little shows where I would actually take the pieces out and I would explain it to people. My aunt happened to know the wife of Mr George Yeo, Minister of Culture at that time. She mentioned that I had this collection which was very interesting and that they should come and visit me. So Mrs Yeo came and she said to her husband, 'Oh

This interest in jewelry led to an intriguing double life as a student and as a jewelry collector.

wow, this is such an interesting story. Why don't you have things like that in the museum?' So George Yeo then rang the museum up and said, 'You should have Mr Chin up as a guest curator and he should curate this jewelry because it's very interesting, it's not just about bling! There's a lot of cultural history and significance to it. So they rang me up and they said 'Would you like to be a guest curator?' I said, 'Oh ok, that's interesting.' Banking really wasn't my thing so I said, it'll take me two years to do this exhibition. Then, I jumped ship which the bank was quite upset about."

"If you try something out and it doesn't work, just try something else!"

HANSON HO

Founder of H55 Design Studio,
Class of 1990

Hanson Ho is the Founder and Creative Director of Singapore-based design firm H55. The firm has been lauded many times over by the British Design and Art Direction (BDAD), New York Type Directors Club, New York One Show Design, Singapore's Creative Circle Awards, Tokyo Type Directors Club, and the New York Art Directors Club. In addition to his work with H55, Hanson has also played the role of curator for the Singapore Land Transport Authority's (LTA) Art-in-Transit Programme for nine Downtown Line MRT Stations. He has been an invited speaker and external examiner for several design institutions, and Head of Design Jury for the Creative Circle Awards, and notably Jury Member for the D&AD Awards. For these, and other achievements, Hanson is a two-time recipient of the President's Design Award, Singapore's highest honour accorded to designers and design projects.

Remarkably, he does not consider any of these feats as an accurate measure of his success. Instead, he values something much more profound: the ability to control his own destiny. "My greatest achievement is to be able to do things on my own terms." As the

> *My greatest achievement is to be able to do things on my own terms.*

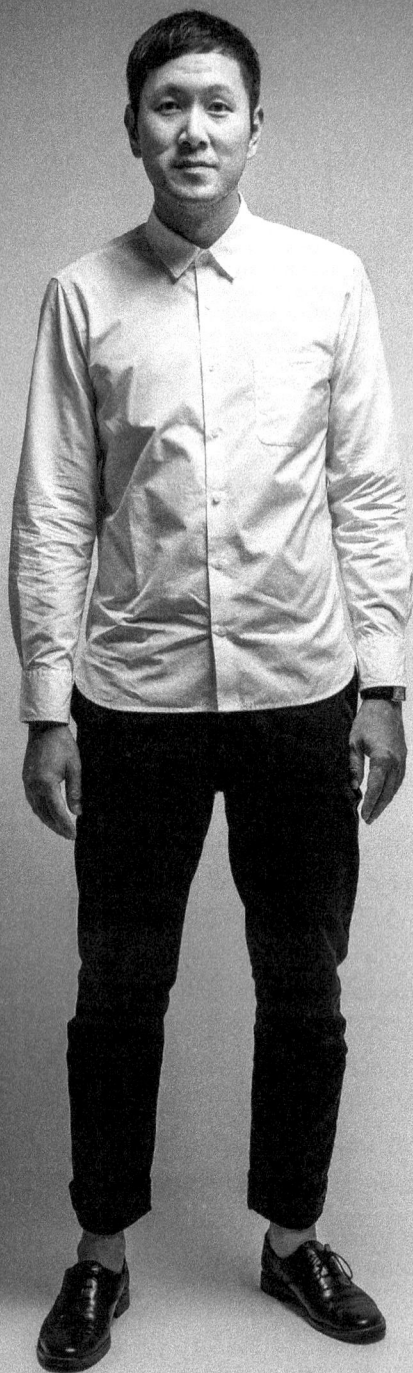

Hanson believes in doing things on his own terms.
[Photo credit to Caleb Ming from Surround]

owner of his own company, Hanson is a living example of what it means to break out of the norm and dare to take charge of one's own future.

From his adolescence, Hanson strived to form his own identity and express himself. This usually involved acts of graffiti on tables, school bags and listening to alternative forms of music. He admits that he was "at a rebellious age" at the time. Thankfully, his quest for self-expression soon morphed into a habit of questioning and pondering about life. He says that his friends in school played a big part in helping him to find himself through their acceptance and open-mindedness. "They would not put on a mask or have any pretence about them. Because of that SJI spirit, everyone felt quite free to speak out and to express themselves."

After Secondary school, Hanson decided to go to a Junior College, a choice that he mildly regrets. "I took the safe path of going to Junior College. After that, I think it occurred to me that it was not really something I wanted to do." His first taste of conformity left a bitter aftertaste. "Parents then had a very fixed mindset of what you should and should not be. We were just going through the system." Soon after, he reversed course and went to a Polytechnic to pursue his passion for design; a practice which was "unpopular and seen as a career that was not lucrative then".

Now, as the head of his own design studio, he actively encourages budding designers to think outside of the box and reject conformity. "Don't be too safe, don't have a fixed mindset." These words sum up his personal philosophy of constantly questioning the system and pushing the boundaries of social norms through his everyday work as a designer.

> " *His friends in school played a big part in helping him to find himself through their acceptance and open-mindedness.* "

Ricky believes that God's blessings have brought him success.

RICKY HO

Composer, Class of 1975

R icky Ho is a prolific composer, conductor and music producer extraordinaire. Ricky's talent and dedication to his craft have won him a number of accolades including his award-winning score for "Seediq Bale — Warriors of the Rainbow" which won him the "Best Original Music Score" at the 48th Golden Horse Awards 2011. He has been nominated four other Golden Horse Awards for his work on Tsui Hark's animation feature "The Chinese Ghost Story", Tsui Hark's "The Legend of Zu", Royston Tan's "12 Lotus" and Chi Po-Lin's "Beyond Beauty". He was also the winner for the "Best Music Score — Gold Remi" in the 47th WorldFest Houston Independent Film Festival 2014 for a documentary feature "Beyond Beauty". In addition, he was awarded the "Best Original Music Score" in the West Hollywood International Film Festival 2008 for "Dance of the Dragon".

He was also a Finalist for "Best Music in a TV Campaign" at the prestigious British Design and Art Direction (BDAD) Awards 2001 for his work on Nippon Paint's "Xinjiang" commercial.

Ricky spent his formative years at SJI where his love for music found fertile ground to grow. "Those days in SJI were just fun! Sports, music and fun; we seldom studied. Because I was already into music at that time, I played music a lot. So we used to gather together, a few of us, classmates, or from other classes, to go jamming. I only started studying three months before the 'O'-levels exams. I still passed though. I was also a sprinter in the athletics team."

In any journey, you need blessings in meeting the right people at the right time to get the right projects.

"Getting into the music industry is very difficult but I was very fortunate. Somehow, everything went smoothly. I got a job at 17, as a professional musician with a band, and then, I decided to move to America and studied music composition. When I came back to Singapore, I was offered a job at a music production company called Music Syndicate. My partner was Iskander Ismail, the composer of the national day songs. Then, we got into the Taiwan market, producing pop music albums and music recordings."

"I believe in God's blessing. So far my life has been good. In any journey, you need blessings in meeting the right people at the right time to get the right projects. Even winning movie awards is very difficult because no matter how good your music sounds, without the right film, you can't win anything. So everything has to come into place. With blessings, it will."

For
COMMUNITY

SJI teachers went out of their way to help students, says Ben.

BEN CHEONG

Founder and Director of Magical Light Foundation,
Class of 1975

Ben Cheong is the Founder and Executive Director of the Magical Light Foundation, a non-profit organisation whose mission is to develop long-term educational programmes and sustainable social development projects for disadvantaged communities in Asia to empower them to be economically independent and to live their life with dignity. He was also actively involved in the disaster recovery missions in Asia including the catastrophic Gorkha Earthquake that killed over 9,000 in Nepal. He also spearheaded a few humanitarian missions to help victims of other recent tragedies in the region. For these, he was nominated as "Singaporean of the Year" in 2015 for his Philanthropy work.

Recounting his days at SJI, he said "I grew up slightly more privileged than some of my classmates, so I did not really understand the concept of being poor as most of my close friends stayed in the kampong. After school I would play with my friends and even thought it was rather cool to stay in the kampong — climbing trees, catching fishes in the pond or drain, making our own toys and games from recycled materials, lighting the kerosene lamps,

> **"**
> *I grew up slightly more privileged than some of my classmates, so I did not really understand the concept of being poor as most of my close friends stayed in the kampong.*
> **"**

drawing water from the well and especially appreciating the friendliness of the kampong spirit. Till today, many of my schoolmates are still in close contact. This enduring spirit of comradeship came from the Josephian values that our teachers imparted to us. Many teachers have made a difference in our lives and those lasting impressions have molded me to be a more caring and compassionate person. Their sense of responsibility to guide, groom and draw out the best in us was always their pride and many even went out of their way and showed kindness and compassion to those who needed it. I recall one incident; my close friend ran away from home in the middle of the night due to some complicated problems at home. We went with him to our teacher's house to seek his advice; our teacher took him in for the night, even though it was against the protocol of teachers to let students stay over. The teacher informed his parents and even mediated with his family to resolve the issue. SJI has given me many important experiences that have positively impacted my life and instilled the right values in me."

Ben was a gemstones trader and a businessman; in his late 40s, things suddenly changed during one of his travels that made him give up everything and concentrate on doing charity full time. He recalled, "I went to Myanmar on holiday and realised that there was no school in thousands of villages. I decided to fund and build a school in one of these villages." In those years, to reach a remote village, he had to take two flights, take a four-wheel drive car on unkind terrains, a sampan to cross the river then had to change to a motorbike to get to the village. This journey took him four days to get to the village. During his first school opening ceremony, the village chief said to him, "I have waited 30 years for you to appear." This brought tears to his eyes and was the turning point when he decided to be a champion in

> **In those years, to reach a remote village, he had to take two flights, take a four-wheel drive car on unkind terrains, a sampan to cross the river then had to change to a motorbike to get to the village.**

bringing education to remote villages across Asia. He feels that education should not be a luxury but a basic human right for all. Ben has not looked back since his first school building project. The Magical Light Foundation which he founded has raised funds to build over 40 schools, over 20 computers labs, over 10 libraries and two medical centres across 10 countries in Asia and continues to serve the poor.

"I believe that you need not be rich or famous to reach out to help fellow human beings that are less fortunate than us. Any ordinary person can become extraordinary because he dares to use his heart to feel the pain of those whose hearts feel no hope, his eyes to see those whose eyes have been shaded by injustice and his hands to reach out to help those whose hands have been handicapped by poverty."

> *I believe that you need not be rich or famous to reach out to help fellow human beings that are less fortunate than us.*

Gerard with some of his young charges at Beyond Social Services.

GERARD EE HUCK LIAN

Executive Director of Beyond Social Services,
Class of 1977

"They could've suspended or caned all of us but they didn't, they tried to understand what exactly the issue was and how they could actually get us to cooperate with the teachers, and that kind of thing... I really appreciated that about SJI." Hailing from the class of 1977, Gerard Ee has transitioned from the rebellious and playful teenager during his time in SJI to become a veteran social worker with an important mission — to help low-income families break out of the poverty cycle. Gerard recalls SJI, speaking with nostalgia about the times when he got into trouble as well as the times when he ate at the stall across the road with friends from different classes and levels. Describing it as a school "that brought everyone together", Gerard is proud of his Josephian heritage. More importantly, Gerard remembers with great respect the caring and understanding teachers in SJI who have helped to shape him into who he is today.

"What I appreciated about SJI was that we had a lot of classes back then. So you had kids that were very smart and some that were average. We had 13 or 14 classes and everyone were friends across the

> " *They could've suspended or caned all of us but they didn't, they tried to understand what exactly the issue was and how they could actually get us to cooperate with the teachers.* "

different classes and sports was a very big thing that united everybody. Every time there was a game, everyone would go down regardless of which class they came from and it was good fun. One of the things that struck me about SJI was that in Secondary 3 my class got in a bit of trouble. Being awkward teenagers, we couldn't cope with the huge jump from Sec 2 to Sec 3 — the switching of streams and the new form teacher. We were always getting into trouble with him and all. But what I appreciated then, was that when I was sent to 'detention', it was actually a means for teachers to build relationships and let troublemakers see that there can be cooperation in a more peaceful way. Looking back, it was quite an enlightened way of resolving a conflict, which is related to what I do as problem de-escalation. They could've suspended or caned all of us but they didn't, they tried to understand what exactly the issue was and how they could actually get us to cooperate with the teachers, and that kind of thing...I really appreciated that about SJI."

"There was always some sort of mutual respect between the teachers and the pupils. One of the reasons was because the teachers did not talk to us like kids but like adults and it didn't feel like they were talking down to us or anything like that."

"SJI was always different. I remember once when most of us were coming late to school, instead of punishing us, I remember that they started some music performances earlier before school so you could come and support your friend who's playing guitar on the stage, so you'll try to wake up and get to school earlier. I thought it was good and I took it for granted back then. Actually it's quite special now that you're older and look back on it."

> 66
> *But what I appreciated then, was that when I was sent to 'detention', it was actually a means for teachers to build relationships and let trouble-makers see that there can be cooperation in a more peaceful way.*
> 99

Mohamed Fareez bin Mohamed Fahmy

Senior Assistant Director,
Family Service Centres (Central),
Class of 1997

Gambling, drug addiction and alcoholism — Fareez has seen it all. As the Senior Assistant Director at a Family Service Centre, Fareez has had the opportunity to touch the lives of thousands of individuals. His dedication to this vocation earned him the Prime Minister's Social Service Award conferred by the National Council of Social Services in 2012. He affirms that SJI played a significant role in shaping his career.

For Fareez, his friends and teachers lived out the SJI Spirit.

"I was someone who came from a low-income family. So when I was in SJI, one of the struggles I had was not having enough money daily. But I had one friend whom I was very close with from Sec 1 all the way to Sec 4. He was someone who always made sure that I had enough food to eat. Like when we went out he would always *belanja*[1] me. He was very supportive, and I think he embodied the SJI spirit of keeping the brotherhood. We supported each other and cared for people with difficulties. So, he's someone whom I am very good friends with, even though he is now based in London. Sometimes i will visit him."

> ❝
> *I think he embodied the SJI spirit of keeping the brotherhood.*
> ❞

[1] Malay word for treat.

Fareez receiving the Promising Social Worker Award in 2011.

Fareez with some of the beneficiaries of the Family Service Centre.

Is there a particular teacher who stands out in your memory?

Ms Daisy Chia taught me for four years. In Sec 1 and 2, she was my Literature teacher and she was my form tutor in Sec 3 and 4. She's very nice. When I first came in Sec 1, I think she was just a new teacher who just started out. She's someone who tries to make her classes interesting and she also shares her stories about her own struggles in life as well. I was in Sec 3 or Sec 4 when my father passed away. During that period, she was there to support me and she also gave me some words of wisdom about her own life experiences and she also gave me space to take my time to adjust back to school during that period. On the day my father passed away, she waited with me while I waited for my mom to fetch me to the hospital. She was always there for me.

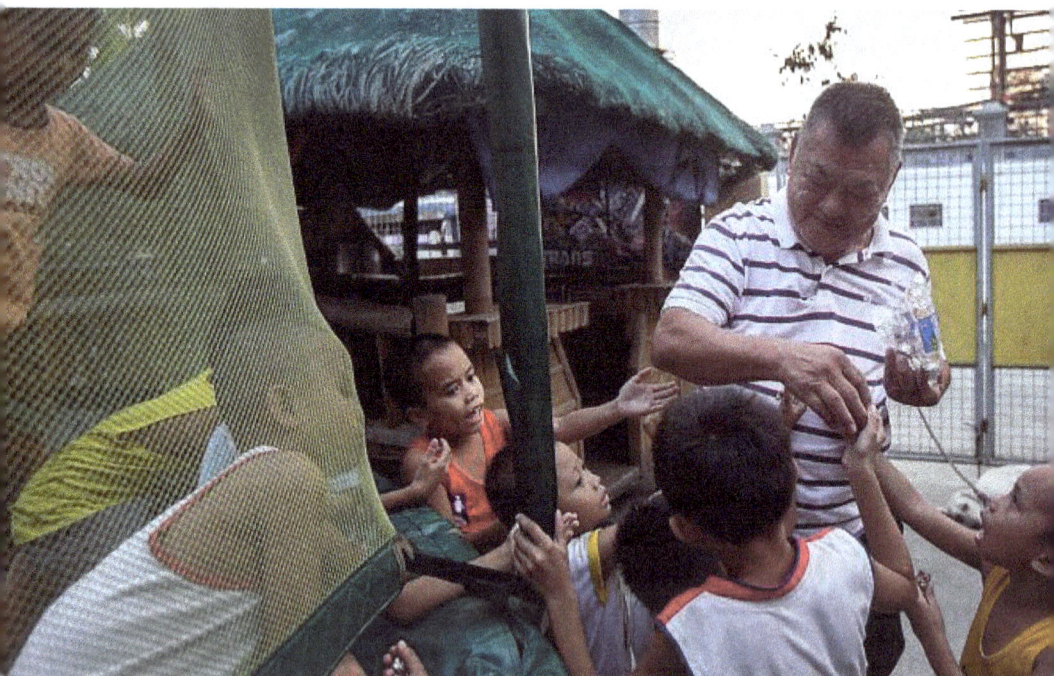

Thomas at the Willing Hearts Orphanage in the Philippines.

THOMAS WEE

Founder of Willing Hearts Orphanage,
Class of 1957

Thomas Wee was the owner of three hotels before he decided to sell it all off, give it all up and dedicate his time entirely to the poor.

"I started this orphanage after my Filipino maid left after working for 15 years. After she left, her sister came back and worked for me. Every month she asked me to send things, so I sent clothing, canned food and electronic items which would weigh more than 50 kg. Then I started thinking about why the family consumes so much. So, I went on a trip with my family to visit them and see where my donations were going. It was a surprise when I saw so many people crammed in one house. Many people were homeless. So, I decided I needed to do something for them. So, I decided to make a U-turn. I had been running hotels, living the good life. I decided to sell all my stuff and change my fate by committing full time to this cause."

> *So, I decided I needed to do something for them. So, I decided to make a U-turn. I had been running hotels, living the good life.*

"SJI has been my mentor, because of the motto 'Ora et Labora'. At that time, the first lesson in the morning was our Catholic class and our weekly Friday confession. I think from those religious teachings, we learnt much more than going to Sunday school. Some time after I left school, is when I went astray. Making money was my only objective. But even though I went astray, I still attended church regularly. I was also a member of this group where I was fully involved in apostolic work. I think the school has done a lot. My father, my son, my grandson and I have all gone to SJI."

For
COUNTRY

SJI kept Joshua on the straight and narrow path.

JOSHUA SOH

—◆—

CEO of HealthSTATS International, Class of 1986

Joshua Soh is currently CEO of Med-tech company HealthSTATS International. His previous positions in the tech industry include Executive Director at ACE, Managing Director at Cisco Systems in Singapore and Brunei, and a variety of managerial positions during his 12 years at IBM. Joshua shares his extensive expertise in IT and management by volunteering to sit on the Board of Governors for the Institute of Technical Education. He also sits on the Government-appointed Committee on the Future Economy.

"I came from a pretty dysfunctional family. My parents were forever fighting. At the end of Primary 1, my parents hit splitsville. That's when Brother Dennis Watt came into the picture. At that time, Brother Dennis was the principal of SJI and St. Michael's School. He understood my situation and was very supportive of my complicated circumstances. Despite all this upheaval, what kept me on the straight and narrow path was Mrs Sheares and dear Brother Dennis and my godparents; they kept me in check. After I finished PSLE, when I was collecting results, you need to imagine that most kids

> **"**
> *What kept me on the straight and narrow path was Mrs Sheares and dear Brother Dennis and my godparents; they kept me in check.*
> **"**

would show up with their parents, I was there alone; very independent. Brother Dennis saw me and asked me, 'How did you do?' And I said, 'Like this la.' He asked where I planned to go. I said, 'SJI of course, right?' He said, 'Come into my office.' He scribbled a few lines on a memo pad, put the slip into an envelope and addressed it to Brother Dominic and he said, 'Just hang onto this and when you get to SJI, just pass this to Brother Dominic.' Shortly after that, I got the posting. The life before SJI was upheaval."

> ## The life before SJI was upheaval.

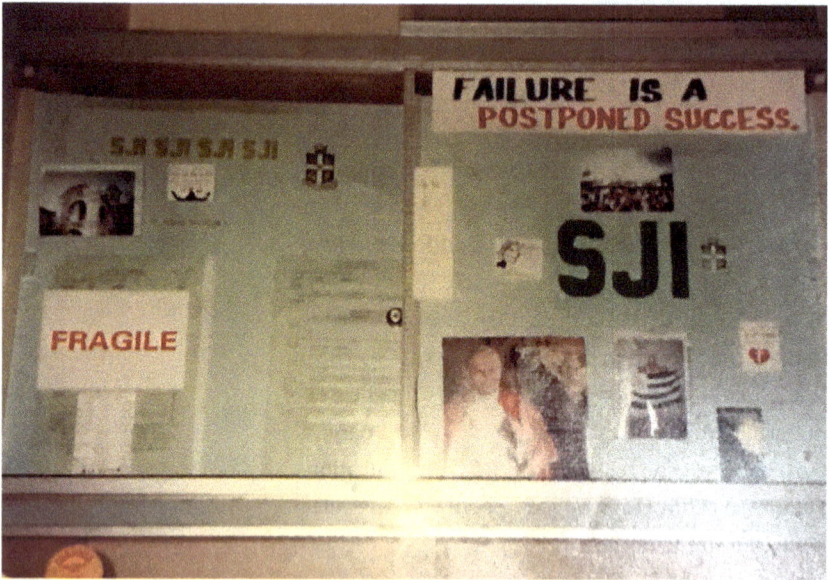

Joshua's Locker at SJI. The quote at the top kept him going, he says. Note his other inspirations too.

"I did what was then known as the Normal stream, so I did Sec 5. The first time I did my O-Level, I did so brilliantly well I scored 21 points. I had always been in a Lasallian setting where you're really quite shielded. So when I first went to a Pre-U Centre, the classroom dynamics were shocking for me. My form tutor couldn't speak proper English so it was very alarming. After that day, I went down to the public phone and I called SJI. I called Brother Joseph and told him it's not gonna work and I need to repeat. The school was really packed then but

Brother Joe just told me, 'Sure come back tomorrow.' They did whatever they had to do with MOE to get me back in."

"I was very involved with the late Mr Peter De Rosa and the sports secretary doing a lot of things. Every time it came to National Day, I would go around the school to put up the flags and the decorations. I just enjoyed doing stuff like that — so anything and everything! I was just really very very involved which made me pretty visible as well."

"Math was where I really struggled. Mr Lee Hwee Kian was my Physics teacher when I first sat for my O-Level and the year that I repeated, he became my Math teacher. He was one of those who had a huge influence on my life. Somehow, with him, there was a rapport and I could just click with him and when he explained, I could absorb and understand. So that year, when he explained Math, I began to enjoy it."

Michael with former President Dr Tony Tan at a Lasallian anniversary event.

MICHAEL SNG

CEO and Managing Partner of TAEL Partners,
Class of 1975

Michael Sng is the Managing Partner and CEO of TAEL Partners, a private equity fund with over US$1.3 billion of assets under management, partnering with business owners in ASEAN. Prior to establishing TAEL Partners, Michael had worked for UOB Asia as its Managing Director and Schroders Singapore.

He was the President of the SJI Old Boys' Association (SJIOBA) for two terms from 2003 to 2007 and appointed to serve on the SJI Board of Governors for 10 years in various positions including Chairman of the Finance and Strategic Finance Committees, and recently as Chair of fund-raising Committee for the redeveloped campus at Malcolm Road.

Michael is also the Founding Governor of SJI International in Singapore. He initiated and led the Lasallian community to establish the newest Lasallian school, SJI International Malaysia and is its Founding Chairman.

Michael (second from right) with his scout troop mates.

> It was my four years in SJI which hold the fondest memories for me — particularly my time spent in the 2103 Hippo Scout Group.

"I come from a family of Josephians. My father, brother, cousins and uncles all studied in SJI. Having experienced firsthand what it means to be a Josephian, I sent two of my sons, Mark and Andre, to study in SJI. But my Lasallian journey began earlier in St. Anthony's Boys' School, from where I went on to SJI for four years before enrolling as the second batch of students in CJC."

"It was my four years in SJI which hold the fondest memories for me — particularly my time spent in the 2103 Hippo Scout Group. Our lives in SJI were made more 'alive' because of this involvement outside the classroom, and I thoroughly enjoyed camping (in Sarimbun and Lim Teck Lee's campsite in Paris Ris). It was evident to me that I did not have the intellectual calibre to be invited to the Istana as a President's Scholar, so I strived to be a President's Scout instead. After moving on to CJC, I returned to SJI to serve in the scouts for many years as a scout leader like many Hippo scouts before me, ensuring that life lessons and skills continued to be passed on to new batches of scouts. We were obviously devastated when the school closed down the scout troop."

"My time in SJI definitely helped me to become who I am today. In SJI we learned how to mix around with all kinds of people, from the very smart boys to the rascals of the school, different people from different races and religions; there was no 'class' distinction — we were colour and class blind. In fact, through socialising and the emphasis on our school values, we somehow embraced the concept of sincerity and empathy — and 'EQ' — one can tell an SJI boy from one who isn't because of our Lasallian values. These values are not just slogans or motherhood statements but *practised* in our daily lives. This has proven to be useful in my later years, where I find myself befriending people unreservedly. It's not about privileges or friendships with benefits, it's about being there for others."

> *One can tell an SJI boy from one who isn't because of our Lasallian values.*

> *It's not about privileges or friendships with benefits, it's about being there for others.*

Noel was appointed as Chief Commando Officer from 1999 to 2003.

NOEL CHEAH

*Chief Operating Officer,
National University Hospital,
Class of 1975*

Noel Cheah is currently the chief operating officer of National University Hospital (NUH), Singapore. Before joining NUH, he pursued a career in the SAF, where he held various leadership and staff appointments, including training the SAF Commandos as the Chief Commando Officer. In addition to undergoing SAF leadership and Commando training courses, he was trained as an officer-cadet on an SAF overseas training award with the German Armed Forces and also attended a staff officer course conducted by the New Zealand Defence Force. During his SAF career, he was awarded the Public Administration Medal (Military).

As a student at SJI, he was a school prefect and represented SJI and combined schools in both football and track and field, and was later selected for the national football team. His best memories of SJI are the friendships he made which last till today. He acknowledges that the opportunities to play sports and represent SJI were a very good experience, and left a lasting impression on him in terms of values like teamwork, esprit de corps and fighting spirit.

> *The opportunities to play sports and represent SJI were a very good experience, and left a lasting impression on him in terms of values like teamwork, esprit de corps and fighting spirit.*

Noel with the SJI Prefects of 1975 (second last row, third from right).

"One must have 'self-belief' and to pursue one's beliefs. I want to add that we must have passion in our pursuits, whatever they may be. And while we pursue our aspirations and beliefs we must always be grounded in our values. Most importantly, one must always be mindful that in whatever we pursue, it must not be for selfish personal gains but must always in one way or another, contribute back to society, the country and the greater good of our fellow man."

Noel reviewing the Guard of Honour at an SJI Annual Parade.

Noel hosting the Brunei Sultan on a visit to HQ Commando and taking a drive in the Light Strike Vehicle — during his appointment as Chief Commando Officer.

Noel (right) with the first President of the Senior Section Student Council, Jeramiah Elijah Lim.

NOEL HON

Former Chairman of E-cop & NEC Asia Pte Ltd,
Former Chairman of the Board of Governors, SJI,
Class of 1962

Noel Hon completed his primary and secondary education at SJI and graduated in 1962 after his O-Levels. He completed his tertiary education at the University of Singapore where he received a Bachelor of Science (Honours) in Physics and a Postgraduate Diploma in Business Administration. He is the former Chairman of e-Cop Pte Ltd.

Over the years, Noel has been an active contributor to the field of Information and Communications Technology. He was Chairman of the Singapore Information Technology Federation, President of the Asian-Oceanian Computer Industry Organization, and President of the Association of Telecommunications Equipment Suppliers. He was also a member of the National Computer Board, the NUS Council, the NIE Council and sat on a number of committees that directed the ascent of Information Technology in Singapore. He was also Chairman of the Singapore Kindness Movement and Chairman of the National Grid Advisory Council. For his contributions to IT, Noel was awarded the Public Service Star in 1991 and the Public Service Star (Bar) in 2003 for his contributions to society.

Noel's contributions are not restricted to the IT field. He was Chairman of the Board of Governors of SJI where he spearheaded the negotiations for the Integrated Programme and the International Baccalaureate for SJI. He was also President of the Singapore Scout Association, Chairman of NTUC Media and a board member of the National Council of Social Services, the Public Transport Council and the Youth Olympic Games Organising Committee. Noel also chaired the Committee for the Redevelopment of the Novena Church. He found this most satisfying, as the Novena Church has been a place of refuge, peace and solace for him over the years.

For him, scouting at SJI played an integral part in his development:

"The thing that really sticks in my mind is my scouting days in SJI. I was in the Scouts and I met a lot of people there and we worked together really well. We were good friends and we still see each other now. Whenever we meet, we are bonded by the principles of scouting. Scouting brings out the best in boys. It teaches them resilience and to abide by the Scouting Honour and the Scout Promise. These things are never forgotten."

"The important thing is that a Scout's Honour is about contributing to the country and helping other people. Also as a scout, you have to always be prepared for all eventualities. It is in truth an international brotherhood. It doesn't mean that all scouts are angels. But the brotherhood between scouts is something that is very, very strong. I think such principles are very necessary."

> 66
>
> *Scouting brings out the best in boys. It teaches them resilience and to abide by the Scouting Honour and the Scout Promise.*
>
> 99

Of his various appointments, his Chairmanship of the ComCare Enterprise Fund is something that is very close to his heart:

"The ComCare Enterprise Fund looks into the funding of social enterprises. It is mainly to fund social enterprises that hire marginalised people. These could be ex-offenders, single mothers etc. This gives them a job and a chance so that they can take responsibility for their own lives rather than depend on charity. When you earn your own money, you earn dignity. With dignity, you can hold your head up high and you become a different person altogether."

> *When you earn your own money, you earn dignity. With dignity, you can hold your head up high and you become a different person altogether.*

Paul is a soldier and a scholar whose desire to serve others guides his life.

PAUL CHEW

Director of Military Security Department, MINDEF, Class of 1988

B rigadier General Paul Chew formally began his SAF career in 1996 upon graduating with a Master's in Aeronautical Engineering from Imperial College, London, under an SAF Scholarship. Since then, Paul has held a diverse range of senior command and staff appointments in the SAF, before assuming his current position as Director of the Military Security Department in 2014. He was also given the opportunity during his military career to further his studies through various sponsorship programmes by the SAF. Paul obtained a Masters in Systems Engineering at the US Naval Postgraduate School (2000) and the Nanyang Fellows MBA pro-gramme at the Nanyang Technological University (2008). For his service to the nation, he was awarded the Public Administration Medal (Bronze) (Military) in 2013.

"I was brought up in a family of SJI boys — my father and step-brothers (all 5 of them) were from SJI. My dad was once a Catholic but he strayed. I was not born Catholic but I became one while in SJI. My sister and I were influenced by my SJI friends to attend catechism and shortly after we were baptised. Our dad decided to go for confession and back to

Catholicism as well."

"But as time passed, I started attending church less. You have stupid reasons like being in a foreign country and you start to stray a little. That was until I met my wife shortly after graduation in 1997. She is a Methodist Christian and we got married in 1998. I became a Methodist and our family now goes to a Methodist church. It is actually the same God — just a different approach to religion."

"My wife and I served in our church choir for a few years until we moved to our current church which is nearer to our home. In my current church, I volunteered to help lead worship songs during Sunday service. My family also joined a Bible study group which we are still members of today. I was also asked to help organise our annual Church Camp in 2015 as the Camp Commandant and the following year as Camp Chairman. I took up the challenge as I believed that God was asking me to step up to play a bigger role in helping our church especially after He had blessed me with a promotion."

Paul's volunteering efforts extend beyond his church:

"Every department in MINDEF adopts a charity organisation. For my department, we adopted a Muslim children's charity — Pertapis Children Home. We encourage and help the kids by playing with them, bringing them to the movies, painting their homes and buying necessities with money from our own pockets. Having my department participate in such acts of service can also help inculcate values such as servanthood and humility, which are important values even as society becomes more affluent, individualistic and self-centered."

"

We encourage and help the kids by playing with them, bringing them to the movies, painting their homes and buying necessities with money from our own pockets.

"

Paul reflects that "when you enter a working environment, personality and character are more important than academic results. This is especially so if one aspires to take on leadership positions in their career. The SAF has molded my character, just like SJI did and I appreciate what they have done for me. I was fortunate to have worked with bosses who had good values and who were willing to spend time coaching and grooming me. Now that I am in a position to also groom others, I will make sure I do the same for my subordinates."

"We must remember that the decisions we make will affect those under us. Everything is in service to others, rather than yourself. This is what has stayed with me all my years in SAF."

> *The SAF has molded my character, just like SJI did and I appreciate what they have done for me.*

Tee How (centre) attending a function at IRAS in August 2015.

TAN TEE HOW

∙∾∙

A Lifetime of Public Service,
Class of 1975

Tan Tee How calls himself an accidental civil servant. "I did not know what the civil service does and what being a civil servant entails." But taking the advice his Sec 4 form teacher, Mr Dominic Yip, had given him before he left SJI, he signed up for a government scholarship, so that he could attend university without having his parents worry about the cost of his education. Upon graduation from NUS in 1983, he started serving out his scholarship bond, thus embarking on a public service career which lasted 34 years.

He held various public service appointments, including that of Controller of Immigration, and Principal Private Secretary to then PM Goh Chok Tong. As founding CEO of the National Healthcare Group from 2000 to 2003, he led the new healthcare network to work closely across all its institutions to deliver seamless, accessible and comprehensive healthcare services. He was appointed Permanent Secretary of the Ministry of National Development (MND) in 2004. Under his leadership, MND agencies embarked on remaking the HDB heartlands, transformed the construction industry to be more forward-looking, and developed the Marina Bay district including Gardens by the Bay. In 2011, he was posted to the Ministry of Home Affairs (MHA). As Permanent Secretary (MHA), he oversaw policies and programmes that contributed to making Singapore safe and secure, spearheaded the reorganisation of the Ministry for greater efficiency and clearer delineation of functions. Under his leadership, a number of major programmes such as the Community Policing programme, Safer Roads Singapore and the Mandatory Aftercare System, were implemented.

As Commissioner of Inland Revenue and Chief Executive Officer of the Inland Revenue Authority of Singapore (IRAS) between 2014 and 2018, he was credited with transforming IRAS and leveraging technology to improve service excellence and make IRAS more taxpayer-friendly. He also played a key role in building new capabilities among IRAS officers, such as in analytics and robotic process automation, to achieve greater efficiency and increase productivity.

He retired from public service on 1 February 2018. Paying tribute to him, Minister in charge of the Civil Service, Deputy Prime Minister Teo Chee Hean said, "He is an effective leader who has made an impactful contribution to the Public Service."

Tan Tee How served in the SJI Board as its Deputy Chairman from 2005 to 2011, during which he played an instrumental role in the design and formulation of the Josephian Programme, which eventually became the SJI International Baccalaureate Integrated Programme. He was also part of a five-person team that spearheaded the formation of SJI International, on whose board he continues to serve till today.

"The Lasallian education has given me a lot of things — friends, my faith and my values. It has made me what I am today. And I share the belief that the Lasallian education still has a lot to offer to Singapore today. I am glad to have had the opportunity to serve my alma mater and contributed towards the work of the Lasallian mission in Singapore."

66
The Lasallian education has given me a lot of things — friends, my faith and my values.
99

Bro. Henry opened Warren's eyes to Shakespeare's world.

WARREN JUDE FERNANDEZ

Editor-in-Chief of The Straits Times,
Class of 1968

Warren Fernandez is Editor-in-Chief of *The Straits Times*, Singapore's largest selling English daily newspaper. He joined the paper in 1990 as a political reporter and rose to become News Editor. He later also served as Foreign Editor and Deputy Editor. He left to join Royal Dutch Shell in 2008 as a Global Manager for its Future Energy project, before returning to the paper in February 2012 as its Editor.

He graduated with First Class Honours from Oxford University, where he read Philosophy, Politics and Economics, and also has a Masters in Public Administration from Harvard University's John F. Kennedy School of Government. Both degrees were obtained on Singapore Press Holdings scholarships.

He has written several books, including *Lee Kuan Yew: The Man and His Ideas*, *Thinking Allowed: Fear, Politics and Change in Singapore*, *Without Fear or Favour: 50 Years of the Public Service Commission*, *Our Homes: 50 Years of Housing a Nation*, *Men for Others*, and most recently, *Lead Your Life!* He was also part of the editorial team that assisted Mr Lee

Kuan Yew with his two-part memoir, *The Singapore Story*. He is also the Chairman of The Straits Times School Pocket Money Fund.

"The teacher I remember most fondly is Brother Henry who's long gone. He was an Irish brother and he taught some of my relatives and they used to tell me that he was the most fearsome character you could imagine. But by the time he taught me, he was this sweet elderly Irish brother who was really so different from what they had told me. They used to tell me how he used to smack them on their heads and make them stand on the chair but he never did anything of that sort to us. He taught us Literature and English and he was a sweet kindly old man who really got us excited about literature and Shakespeare. So, he opened my mind to that part of the world."

Of his many contributions to society, one of them holds a special place in his heart:

"The ST School Pocket Money Fund is very close to me because it was something that grew ground up. It started when I was at the newsdesk and one of our journalists came up to me and said 'I want to do something for Children's Day.' So we debated it and I said 'Can you narrow your initiative down to what is the most critical need children face, according to the social workers?' So she went away for a few weeks and then she came back and said 'The biggest problem that many kids from poor homes face is so basic — they just don't have money in their pockets when they go to school to buy enough food to keep them from going hungry.' And that crystallised it to its bare essence. So I said 'That's what you should focus on!' So I remember how we launched it in a very simple, rough and ready way. We took about 100 kids from disadvantaged homes to Orchard Cinema for a movie screening, launched it there, and we aimed to help a few hundred kids in our first years.

> " *He taught us Literature and English and he was a sweet kindly old man who really got us excited about literature and Shakespeare. So, he opened my mind to that part of the world.* "

But today, we help 14,000 kids a year, and we have to raise 7 million dollars each year in order to meet that. The success of the ST School Pocket Money Fund is something that we're all very proud of; that we actually took this on and managed to keep it going."

For
EDUCATION

Agnes believes that education is the key to improving one's life.

AGNES CHANG

Associate Professor (Retired),
National Institute of Education,
Class of 1964

D r Agnes Chang completed her pre-university
studies at SJI in 1964 and was in the last intake
of girls at that time. She retired as an Associate
Professor from the National Institute of Education
(NIE), Nanyang Technological University (NTU),
in 2010. Currently she is the academic advisor to The
Kinderland Education Services Pte Ltd and is
teaching Professional Development courses at NIE,
Nanyang Polytechnic, Nanyang Academy of Fine
Arts and the Singapore Teacher's Union. Her key
research areas include employability, thinking,
problem solving, motivation, child development and
bilingualism.

As a teacher in SJI, Agnes was one of the 10
counsellors, advising students on financial, emotional
and social problems.

"I remember two pre-U boys who wished to quit
their studies to work because of financial difficulties
at home. I promised to help them find financial
assistance if they were to do well in their A-Level
exams. I checked on them frequently to give
encouragement. Both did well enough to get PSC

> **Education is the way to improve lives, as it provides people with the tools necessary to help themselves.**

scholarships and are now engineers. They thanked me for 'scolding' them."

Aside from this, Agnes also held additional Saturday classes for her weaker students, that lasted most of the day. Her former students say that she was always willing to go the extra mile to help those who needed it. Agnes is driven by the personal belief that everyone deserves a helping hand, and the chance to succeed in society.

She believes that education is the way to improve lives, as it provides people with the tools necessary to help themselves.

KOH THIAM SENG

Associate Dean at the
National Institute of Education,
Class of 1976

D r Koh Thiam Seng is an alumnus of SJI. A
teacher by profession, he has taught in schools
and has held several senior appointments at the
National Institute of Education (NIE) and the
Ministry of Education (MOE), before returning to
SJI to serve as its principal from 2009 to 2015. At
MOE, he was a Deputy Director involved in policy
formulation for university, polytechnic and ITE
education. As Director of Educational Technology,
he led the implementation of Singapore's 2nd
Infocomm Technology (ICT) in Education
Masterplan. He was also a Deputy Director at NIE
overseeing educational research. Recognised
internationally for his expertise on the use of ICT
for learning, he has served as a consultant to the
Singapore Army, ST Engineering, IDA International
and Intel (US).

At SJI, Thiam Seng worked with the Board of
Governors, staff and other stakeholders to successfully
introduce the Integrated Programme in 2013, a six-
year programme that integrates four years of
secondary education with two years of junior college
education leading to the International Baccalaureate

Thiam Seng (left) sharing a laugh with DPM Teo Chee Hean at an SJI event.

> **I bombed out of everything except for my Maths, where I scored relatively high.**

Diploma. During his term at SJI, he initiated various curricular innovations, including special programmes such as ArtScience and Business Design Thinking and student development initiatives such as self-regulated learning to better prepare the students for the future.

He very fondly remembers his formative years at SJI.

"At that time, classes were huge. Typically, every class had about 40 to 43 students. And I remember during my year we had about 14 classes in Sec 1. In terms of facilities, it was not that great when compared to the facilities at the current SJI. But I think what is probably uniquely SJI is the sense of community. You made very good friends in school, through class activities and through CCA. I was in NCC."

"I was probably the last person to be admitted into the science stream. I was a bit unusual in terms of my studies. I bombed out of everything except for my Maths, where I scored relatively high. Science was okay but the rest I flunked by quite a fair bit. But I had a science teacher, Agnes Chang, who saw my Maths grade and thought it was a bit unusual. I believe that she fought for my admission into the science stream. I guess for whatever reason, she thought that scoring 80 odd percent for maths at that time was phenomenal when compared to my other subjects."

"I suppose having gone through SJI in my secondary school years; it would only be fair to say that SJI inculcates in you a sense of giving back. And I suppose I became a teacher because I felt that it was a way of giving back. Along the way, I went on to teach at the Institute of Education which needed someone to teach the use of technology in education. Very few people then in education knew how to use technology, and I happened to have it as a hobby and was fascinated by Apple Computers. As there was an opening in the Institute of Education, my former science teacher, Agnes Chang, who was now a Head of Department at NIE, asked me if I would like to go over to the Institute of Education to teach the use of technology in education!"

"So along that process, I was given the opportunity to do a PhD. They needed a chemistry lecturer in the new university. Since I had a Master's Degree, they decided to send me. At that time IT became very big. Leo Tan, who is also an SJI old boy, was a member of the Ministerial Committee for ICT. And that was how the Ministry got to know me. And eventually they got me to the Ministry Headquarters where I spent about eight years. After that time, when I was about to return to NIE, the Old Boys from the Board of Governors in SJI asked whether I would be prepared to return to SJI as Principal because SJI at that time was facing some challenges. I said 'Yes, I will be happy to serve my Alma Mater.'"

> **Very few people then in education knew how to use technology, and I happened to have it as a hobby and was fascinated by Apple Computers.**

For Levan, life is a prayer.

LEVAN LIM

Head of Early Childhood & Special Needs Education,
National Institute of Education,
Nanyang Technological University,
Class of 1978

A ssociate Professor Levan Lim has worked in various countries, including the United States of America, Australia and Singapore. At the National Institute of Education (NIE), he has taught courses in the Master of Education (Special Education) programme as well as in the Diploma in Special Education (DISE) programme. The DISE programme trains special education teachers for special education schools and Allied Educators (Learning & Behavioural Support) to support students with special needs in mainstream schools. His research interests include the transition and post-school outcomes of students with disabilities; severe disabilities; intentional communities and relationships for persons with disabilities; the inclusion of students with disabilities within mainstream schools; and trends and issues in special education in Singapore. From 2005 till 2009, before he became Head of the Early Childhood & Special Needs Academic Group (ECSE AG) at NIE, he was an executive board member at the Association for Persons with Special Needs (APSN).

The SJI Mission to develop 'men of integrity and men for others' has contributed enormously to aspects of my life, in particular, to the formation and growth of my spiritual faith, which, to me, is my most precious blessing, treasure and gift.

"The SJI Mission to develop 'men of integrity and men for others' has contributed enormously to aspects of my life, in particular, to the formation and growth of my spiritual faith, which, to me, is my most precious blessing, treasure and gift. My gratitude knows no boundary in giving thanks and appreciation to all the Brothers and teachers at St. Michael's (now known as SJI Junior) and SJI, and those before them who planted seeds, touched, inspired and awakened myself and countless other students to the birth and nurturance of the Christian spirit."

"As an Associate Professor at NIE before I became Head of ECSE AG, I engaged in voluntary activities with several Voluntary Welfare Organisations (VWOs) in the disability sector. At APSN, I was chair of the curriculum committee which was responsible for developing transition pathways and curricula for its students. I have also been involved in voluntary capacities with the Down Syndrome Association in an inclusion project for boys with Down Syndrome at SJI Junior as well as in a work conversion project at SPD (formerly known as Society for the Physically Disabled)."

"How I became Head at ECSE AG is interesting. I had gone to Lourdes, France, about a decade ago for a conference in spirituality and disability, a few months after I received my tenure at NIE, NTU. Besides listening to and learning from the conference speakers, such as Jean Vanier (the founder of the L'Arche Communities) and Professor John Swinton, I was also listening and praying within. I was asking God what He had wanted of me, now that I had tenure and asked him to till and loosen the field of my soul so that I could more readily wait and receive God's plan for my life. On Monday morning at NIE, after my return to Singapore over the weekend, my Dean called to meet me to ask about becoming the next Head of ECSE AG. It's like Ora et Labora, prayer and work, working in unison within our lives to guide our life directions and journeys. Actually, thinking about this for some time, I also see work, how we consecrate it, how we treat others at work — in essence, how we live our lives at work — as a form of prayer. It's not just Ora et Labora, it's also Labora est Ora (to work is to pray)."

> " *I also see work ... as a form of prayer.* "

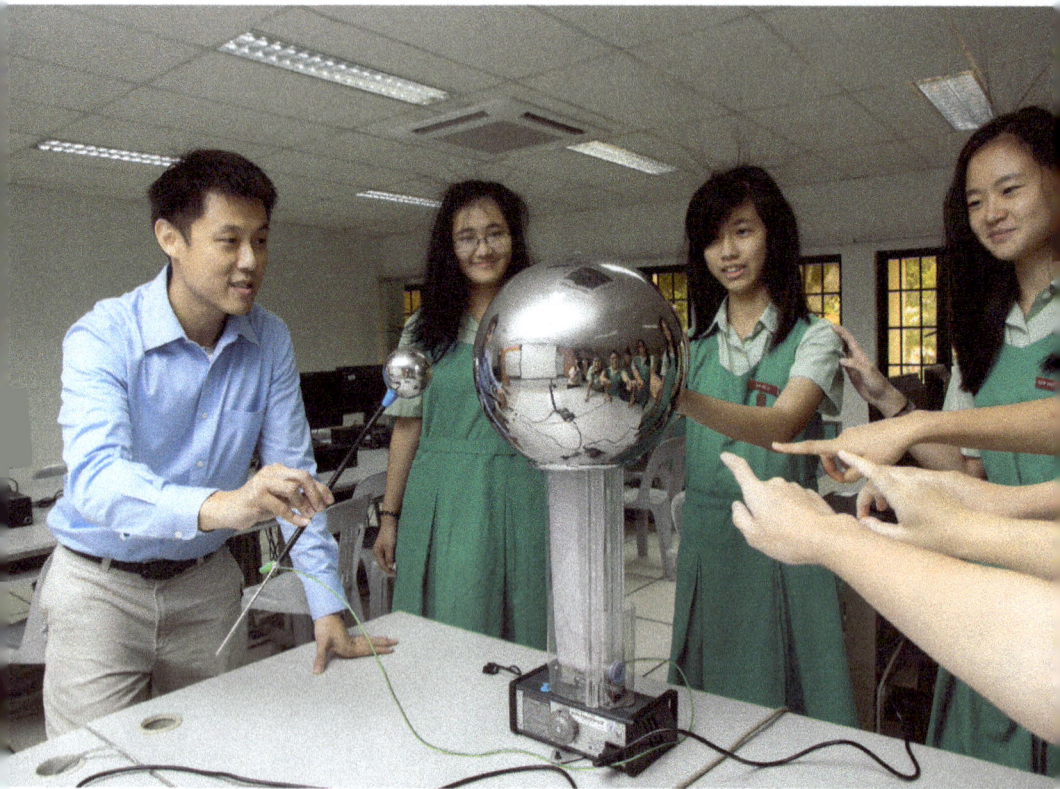

Boon Chien was inspired by his SJI teachers to celebrate success with his own students.

YAP BOON CHIEN

President's Award for Teachers 2012,
Class of 1989

Yap Boon Chien is a Physics Master Teacher at the Academy of Singapore Teachers, a pedagogical leader and a mentor in a wider education community. It is his desire to grow a fraternity of Teacher Leaders with a passion for educating students to enjoy learning and put in their personal best to contribute to society. Boon Chien makes innovative use of gadgets, demonstrations and concrete experiences to draw his students into the abstract concepts of Physics. His use of experiential lessons enhances student engagement and arouses their curiosity. Boon Chien believes firmly in the correlation between student motivation and learning; he role-models and instils values such as resilience in learning through motivational talks and regular dialogues.

His pedagogical contributions at the school, cluster and national levels have been recognised with numerous awards, including the President's Award for Teachers in 2012. He is also the recipient of the Southeast Asian Ministers of Education Organization (SEAMEO) Science Teacher Award 2012, winner of the Crescendas Medal and Prize for Outstanding

> ❝ *Boon Chien makes innovative use of gadgets, demonstrations and concrete experiences to draw his students into the abstract concepts of Physics.* ❞

Boon Chien receiving the President's Award for Teachers.

Physics Teacher 2010 (Secondary Schools) awarded by the Institute of Physics, Singapore and recipient of Nanyang Outstanding Young Alumni Award 2013.

"SJI provided Josephians with a very encouraging and nurturing environment; it created many opportunities for us to explore and develop our talents. An impactful event I recalled was during my Secondary 3 Physical Fitness test. At the Standing Broad Jump station, to my surprise, I jumped out of the standard markings on the standing broad jump scale! I was not aware of this special talent I had. All my friends from my 3 Science 1 class were clapping and celebrating this unique moment together; the atmosphere was very encouraging and inspiring. My PE teachers, Mr Zehnder and Mr Michael Chia, also marvelled at my jump. Mr Chia placed a few markers (as targets) on the Standing Broad Jump mat and encouraged me to try for my personal best. That day I made a few jumps and managed to achieve a good personal record of 2.85m. Then immediately the PE teachers offered me an opportunity to join in the track and field training that following Saturday. SJI created this environment of a 'celebration of success' for me and my friends. When my classmates did well in either academic or non-academic areas, you witnessed fellow Josephians from even the class next door actually coming by to congratulate them. This is something very unique about that group of Josephians, the 1989 batch. Everyone actually celebrates each other's talents, strengths and successes. So now, this has formed part of my Teaching Philosophy; that every child is unique and special and should be given the right support to bring out the best in them and it is my role as a teacher to awaken these talents and create an environment that celebrates successes together."

> *SJI created this environment of a 'celebration of success' for me and my friends.*

For

GOD

Fr. Vaz preaching at a First Holy Communion Mass at the Parish of St. Teresa's.
[Photo credit to Steven John]

REV MSGR AMBROSE VAZ

Priest, and Vicar General (Pastoral), Class of 1968

Monsignor Ambrose Vaz is the Vicar General (Pastoral) of the Archdiocese of Singapore. The title of Monsignor is granted to individuals who have rendered valuable service to the Church, or who provide some special function in Church governance. As Vicar General, he is the deputy of the Bishop. He attended St. Stephen's Primary School and graduated from SJI in 1968. He was ordained to the priesthood in 1981 and was first posted to the Church of the Holy Cross. His vocation has seen him serve the Archdiocese in a variety of capacities. He has been the Spiritual Director for the Choice Program, the Family Life Society, Catholic Engaged Encounter and Director of the Biblical Apostolate, Formator and Rector of the Major Seminary. Under his able leadership, these programmes have grown very strong over the years, bringing love, joy and peace to thousands for almost 40 years.

What role did SJI play in your life?

I was in SJI from 1965 to 68. What I appreciated most was a very holistic education. Although they encouraged us to have academic excellence, it was very well rounded. I think there was a lot of focus on the moral character of a young teenager. I found that very helpful because you know we were told that we were special; special to God and therefore we were kind of chosen by Him to make a difference in society. So I felt a certain sense of pride. Our Sec 1 teacher made us feel a special love. Being special was not because we were smart, good looking or anything like that but basically because we were blessed by God and so I felt that one thing SJI taught me is to be very grateful; grateful not just to have the chance to be educated, but even more, to be loved to be cared for. I think that shaped the future for me.

> *One thing SJI taught me is to be very grateful.*

We hear that you volunteered to do National Service (NS)?

When I joined the Seminary, it was under the old scheme. Before NS, I joined the Seminary and once you joined the Seminary you were exempted from NS. But we volunteered to do NS. So at that time, they told us, "You are already in the Seminary so you do not need to do NS." But we asked to come out and do it. I told myself, as a priest I am going to help young men who have difficulties; like men who are struggling in NS and if I do not know what it is all about because I have never been there then how would I identify with them. We were the first batch of Seminarians who ever went for NS and the Bishop at that time was very reluctant. But after we did it, we recommended it and said it was very good so it became compulsory. That was in 1973.

> *We were the first batch of Seminarians who ever went for NS and the Bishop at that time was very reluctant.*

Was it hard to go back to the Seminary after NS? Did you have a girlfriend?

I had one special girlfriend at one time and a few others that came and went. But no, I think all along, the focus was still to be fair and honest with them. Before dating them, I told them where I came from before NS and where I may go back to. When we took our break to join NS, we were told that it was as though we had left the Seminary and that there was to be no fear in getting involved with someone; after all, when we came back from NS, we would have to reapply to enter the Seminary. So we were really given the freedom to just be as though we had never joined. So, I would say that, I was exposed to the possibility of being a husband and father, but the call to respond as a priest was stronger.

Do you think SJI played a part in your becoming a priest?

Of course! Besides, in SJI, at that time, we used to have retreats and talks by seminarians. Seminarians would come and chat with us and tell us what their life was like. So, these are the things that connected with my desire to serve. Maybe that is why after my Sec 4 year, I did my pre-U studies in the Seminary. Like I said, I am grateful for what I received at SJI. The whole ethos of gratitude is to try and see whether you can pay back and give similar opportunities to others.

Daniel and his wife, Shirley, meet Pope Francis.

DANIEL EE

*Worldwide Marriage Encounter
International Ecclesial Team,
Class of 1971*

Daniel Ee is a Director at Keppel Infrastructure Fund Management, a listed business trust that invests in infrastructure assets locally and globally. He has been an independent director of various corporations including Citibank Singapore Ltd, SMRT Corporation Ltd, the Civil Aviation Authority and the National Environment Agency since the late 1990s. He spent 10 years in various government organizations and 15 years in investment banking. Outside of his business endeavours, he and his wife together with a priest form the international leadership team of Worldwide Marriage Encounter (WWME), a non-profit Catholic Movement present in 94 countries. WWME conducts programmes that enrich and strengthen marriages and the priesthood.

"What I valued most about SJI was the well-rounded education that I received. There was a good balance of academic and other aspects of school life. At the time, my main ECA (now known as CCA) was the NCC. I was also involved in the Prefectorial Board, the Literary, Debate and Dramatic Society (LDDS), and the Math and Science Society. It stretched me as I had to learn how to manage my

> 66
> *What I valued most about SJI was the well-rounded education that I received.*
> 99

time. The NCC and the Prefectorial Board especially required a lot of time.

"We had some of the best teachers anyone could have had — good teachers of academic subjects and mentors on how to live life. I really benefited from this. And we also had La Salle Brothers — they were a key feature of school life. They were role models

1st Batch of SJI Cadet Lieutenants with the NCOs in 1971. Daniel is in the middle of the front row.

for living life in a more disciplined way because they lived in communities. They didn't own luxuries of any sort yet were very motivated in terms of what they were doing, whether it was teaching or sports. And they were fair and firm in disciplining the boys. So I think SJI gave us a very very good base to start from."

"As a Catholic school, the Catholic ethos came through very strongly. It came through in terms of morning prayers, the catechism sessions we attended, the Brother who taught us religious and moral education. We were constantly reminded that it was not only important for us to do well in our studies but to also make a difference to society — to be able to contribute to society in whatever endeavour that we were involved in."

"My wife Shelley and I have been very involved in both WWME and in our parish. In fact Shelley has been my pillar of strength and is a great partner. We have learnt to strike a balance between what we do for ministry, office and family life. You have asked, 'Why do all these things? Why don't you take it easier?' I think in the end we all want to do things that are meaningful and fulfilling. That happens when we serve others. And that is the lasting legacy of my SJI formation."

> "
>
> *In the end we all want to do things that are meaningful and fulfilling.*
>
> "

Fr. Bosco says that he would encourage anyone to join SJI.

FR. JOHN BOSCO PEREIRA

Priest, Sportsman, Prankster, Class of 1978

Fr. Bosco cuts a striking figure with his clean shaven head and well manicured goatee. His voice is unmistakable and laughter infectious.

As the parish priest of St. Teresa's Church, Chaplain of SGH and Procurator of the Seminary he wears many hats. But wearing several hats is nothing new to the avid sportsman.

"I represented school at that time in soccer, hockey, athletics and cross-country. We were national champs for both Hockey and Soccer and I was on both the winning teams. In 1977, we were champs for the B-division in Hockey. In Sec 1 and Sec 2 we were national champs also, but in the B-division SJI weren't winning the national finals until we won it. Then in 1978, the B-division team were also national champs. I was also in the Scouts, the ELDDS and the Malay Society, so I had my hands full."

"Those were the best years of my life," he recalls with a broad smile. "I have many, many fond memories of being in SJI. My Sec 1 and Sec 2 class, we were basically together, then in Sec 3 we were

> **I represented school at that time in soccer, hockey, athletics and cross-country... I was also in the Scouts, the ELDDS and the Malay Society.**

Fr. Bosco (fourth from the right) with his fellow Officer Cadets.

streamed into different classes. Not too long back we had a little reunion of sorts, and while we were having some drinks, I took one of the little serviettes, and I just started writing the names that I could recall from my class. Believe it or not, I could write down 45 names. So that's how memorable they were, every single one."

Fr. Bosco himself leaves an impression on everyone he meets, not in the least for his terrific sense of humour; a skill honed in his days at SJI. After a little persuasion he reveals to us one of his pranks:

"When we were neighbours with the CHIJ girls, we had what was known as the Math and Science competition. Two classes from SJI, the two top classes that won the internal one would meet the two classes over there, and CHIJ was hosting it. So on stage you have the participants and I was just one of the students cheering them on, but I decided to play a prank over there by creating a little homemade stink bomb. It was in the hall, and I hid it and mixed in everything, and I just left it behind the curtains. It was mayhem! The girls were screaming because of the smell and everything came to a standstill. The prefects were trying to find out who the culprit was, and I had someone who pointed the finger at me. I had to face the music afterwards."

How did a prankster sportstar become a Catholic Priest? "I had the calling since when I was maybe 14 or 15, but I always pushed it or shelved it. Like I said I was pretty active and there were girls on the scene. I did not feel worthy of the call, but it never left me and was still within me. So when I left, graduating from the States, this call was very, very strong. And it was there where I made the decision."

"I have no regrets being at SJI, I will always encourage anyone to go into SJI. I think that the school motto, 'Ora et Labora', says everything. To give your best in everything. To work hard. To play hard. Give a 100 percent in all aspects of the education system. The philosophy of SJI is to be able to mold us, not just into intellects, but into young men who are able to go out to embrace the world."

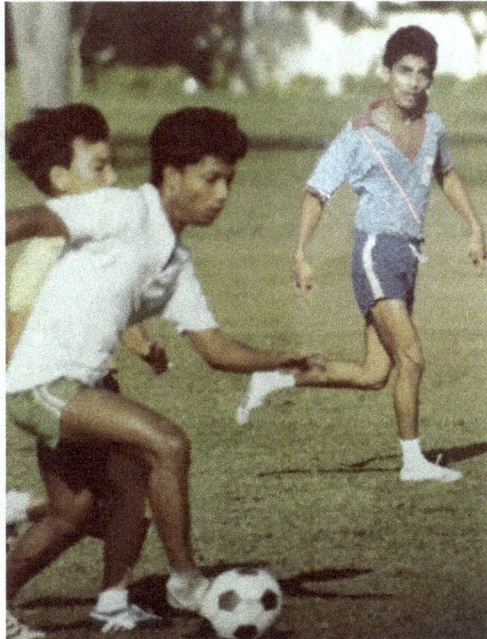

Fr. Bosco dribbling on football pitch in 1978.

Being a member of the Military Band was a big part of Fr. John-Paul's life.

FR. JOHN-PAUL TAN OFM. JCL

Franciscan Priest and Chancellor of the
Catholic Archdiocese of Singapore,
Class of 1977

Friar John-Paul Tan is the Chancellor of the Catholic Archdiocese of Singapore. He is responsible for the Chancery, which is an arm of the Archbishop's offices — collectively known as the Curia — that handles administrative functions such as HR, clergy matters and records management and archives. While this may sound bureaucratic, the focus of the Chancery is keenly pastoral. The primary responsibility of the Chancery is to help the Archdiocese in its administrative functions and governance, and to preserve and safeguard documents for the Church's future. When Archbishop Emeritus Nicholas Chia retired in 2013, his successor, Archbishop William Goh, appointed Franciscan Friar John-Paul Tan, as the Chancellor, a role mandated by canon 482 of the Code of Canon Law. The good friar was well positioned for the role given his extensive experience as Parish Priest of St. Mary of the Angels, Defender of the Bond for the Ecclesiastical Tribunal and as Guardian (Superior) of the Franciscan Houses.

Looking back, what is your best memory of SJI?

Being part of the SJI Military Band! It was good fun with a lot of good friends. A few of us from that period of time became priests! Fr. Leslie Raj (our drum major, from the same year as me), Fr. Anselm Phang (a Carmelite priest), Fr. Joachim Chang (two years my junior, whom I taught the clarinet to). The band took up quite a bit of our time. We had band practice on Saturdays, concert practice and marching practice. Those friendships, they go back, and I continue to keep in touch with the bandsmen.

Would you say that music was an important part of your life as a child?

My sister took up the piano at home, but the first time I took up an instrument was at SJI with the clarinet. I soon got into practising with an orchestra, seeing how all the different instruments come together for performances and marching. In National Service, I was part of the military band and played the first clarinet. It was another level of appreciation being introduced to the whole new world of music.

During your time at SJI, who was your favourite teacher?

There were a few. Mrs Joan Fong was one. She was one who reinforced the Catholic image of SJI, and she was very conscientious about that. I remember there was a Mr Balan in Secondary 2. We were playing up in class, like typical SJI boys. He gave us a good one hour's scolding, about what we wanted to do in life and what the future is about. This woke us up and reminded us that we have to take charge of our lives and what we want out of life. I guess that action did some of us good!

> " The first time I took up an instrument was at SJI with the clarinet. "

During your time at SJI, did you know you wanted to become a priest?

No, absolutely not. In SJI, I wasn't even a Catholic, but I attended Masses. There were also the Lenten vigils which I attended. At Band camp, we had the Masses and prayers. After leaving SJI, I started going to a parish, and it was actually my bandmates who invited me to church. From there, I got baptised, and here I am!

I think the Catholic culture was very significant in SJI. To have a chapel, to have the La Salle Brothers around, to have priests; these are the things that, at a younger age, you thought every school had. When you don't have it, you realise that you miss it.

Would you say the Chapel was your favourite part of school?

No, it was the band room! It was where we hung out.

What advice would you give someone who is considering the priesthood?

Get a life! Yes, what I mean is live life, be passionate about your studies, be passionate about life, with all your interests and hobbies. And then, when you are fully alive as a human person, and God calls you, you can respond with your personality and the totality of who you are. That's what a vocation is about. You don't give up anything by entering the religious life. In fact, you live to the full. If I didn't think I was going to live my life to the full, I wouldn't have joined anyway. We only have one life each, why waste it? If this was it, and it would bring me purpose and meaning, go for it! I didn't see religious life as a giving up or a sacrifice. Many people do, but it shouldn't be seen as a sacrifice.

> "
> *In SJI, I wasn't even a Catholic, but I attended Masses.*
> "

A historian by training, Bro. Mike believes he might have become an archivist if not for the calling.

BRO. MICHAEL BROUGHTON

Vice President for Lasallian Mission,
De La Salle University Manila,
Class of 1971/73

B ro. Mike as he is affectionately known is a familiar figure to the SJI family. He studied at both St. Michael's School and De La Salle School before moving on to and completing his 'O' and 'A' Levels at SJI. After completing his national service (infantry section leader) and university education in English and History & Politics at the University of Singapore, he returned to teach at his beloved alma mater in 1979. His zeal for education eventually led to his appointment as Deputy Principal for Student Development at SJI in 1990. Under his dynamic leadership, significant changes were wrought, gradually shifting the paradigm on co-curricular activities. SJI's status as a forerunner in Character Development is due in large part to Bro. Mike's efforts.

"Back when Mr Patrick Zehnder was Sports Secretary, SJI always attended the annual National Track and Field Meet," Bro. Mike recalls. "As one of the top four schools, we were allowed to bring a thousand students as supporters, but SJI never brought a thousand supporters for any track and field event. Some teachers complained, 'If we go there,

> " *As one of the top four schools, we were allowed to bring a thousand students as supporters.* "

what will we do?' I said, 'We can cheer.'"

Bro. Mike also supported the revival of the House System, sending two houses at a time to the track and field meet to cheer. "SJI was not a cheering school then, unlike schools such as Raffles Girls School, whose cheers could bring the house down! However, that had to change. When the track and field meet arrived, we sent two houses to the event, numbering approximately a thousand students together, and they would cheer. All together. By heart, every single SJI cheer. And they could do it, with just one signal from their House Cheer Leaders!"

"At every national sports event, we would continue to send one House to be present and cheer for SJI. We could do that because the culture of the school had grown from a non-cheering, non-singing one to become a school which could cheer and sing enthusiastically with confidence. These songs evoke strong levels of emotion and this is what bonds students together — the powerful feelings and emotions expressed through our unique songs and chants. This culture of participation binds us together as one SJI community."

> Interestingly, I realise some of the most loyal people to the school were from the uniformed groups.

Bro. Mike's passion for SJI is undeniable. He attributes this passion to his ties with the Military Band. "I was part of the military band when I was a student. Interestingly, I realise some of the most loyal people to the school were from the uniformed groups. Our band instilled a sense of intense pride for the school within its members, and this allowed them to be fully associated with the school culture. I believe belonging to something is important to develop fully as a Josephian. If you choose to roll right through SJI, without belonging to anything, or making any commitment to any group, you will gain less from your years in this school. This sense of fellowship and belonging is one of the things which guided me in my decision to become a Brother for the Lasallian mission, helping and educating others with my fellow Brothers."

With a passion for history and story-telling, Bro. Mike reckons that if he had not chosen to become a Brother and educator, he would have likely become an archivist. In his years at SJI, he embarked on a personal project to find out as much information as possible about all the La Salle Brothers who had passed away on Singapore soil. As a result of his efforts, he managed to inscribe the names, birth and death years of all the brothers who had passed away on plaques which used to hang on the walls of the chapel at the Malcolm Road campus. "I wanted to ensure that the memory of all who had contributed to the Lasallian mission and history would be remembered and future Josephians can learn from the efforts of our predecessors and become truly Men for Others."

It is said that those who lead others unto righteousness, shall shine like stars forever. Bro. Mike's star shines brightly for those who have been blessed to come into his orbit.

> *I wanted to ensure that the memory of all who had contributed to the Lasallian mission and history would be remembered and future Josephians can learn from the efforts of our predecessors and become truly Men for Others.*

For

JUSTICE

The seeds of his legal career were perhaps sown at SJI, says Justice Chan Seng Onn.

CHAN SENG ONN

Judge of the High Court of Singapore and
President of the Industrial Arbitration Court,
Class of 1972

Justice Chan Seng Onn never considered a legal career until somewhat later in life. Seng Onn is the recipient of the 1973 President's Scholarship and Colombo Plan Scholarship. In 1976 he graduated with First Class Honours from University College London in Engineering and received the A.P. Head Medal, the Highest Engineering Award for being the top student in the Faculty of Engineering. He also received the Goldsmid Medal for being the best student in the Naval Architecture/Mechanical Engineering Course in the University College London. "I went to University College London under a scholarship to study Naval Architecture, after which I was posted to the Navy. At the time when I finished school, the only thought in my mind was that I would become an engineer and nothing less," recalls Seng Onn. It was only 10 years later that he received his Bachelor of Laws degree from the University of Singapore and that was achieved under the auspices of the PSC Legal Training Scholarship.

But the roots of his legal career were perhaps sown at SJI. Beyond his success in the science courses at SJI, Seng Onn won the Aquila shield in 1970 for

> **66**
>
> *The roots of his legal career were perhaps sown at SJI.*
>
> **99**

the best English essay, much to the surprise (and horror, he says) of his batch mates who did not see him as being that proficient in English. "In fact, it was totally unexpected," he recalls. His conclusion? "Life has its own quirks. As it turns out, I really do like my present job, which is something totally unexpected, I would never have dreamt of it."

But whether coincidence or fate would have it, what Seng Onn learnt in SJI provided his moral compass in life. "I think the Christian values of a sense of justice, sense of right and wrong and how to be a good person are the things they have, as a Christian Brother School, cultivated in their students," he remarks about SJI. "I was not from a well-to-do background but I was given the chance to develop. You did not feel small in any way just because of your background."

Before Seng Onn became a judge, he had served in many occupations in the public service. Out of these many occupations, those that he felt most rewarding were that as Deputy Public Prosecutor and his present post as judge. "As a Deputy Public Prosecutor, you derive a fulfillment and satisfaction from seeing that justice is done."

When asked which of his SJI experiences proved to be most useful in life, he emphatically declares "Ora et Labora!"

> *SJI provided his moral compass in life.*

CHRISTOPHER BRIDGES

———— ⸿ ————

Litigator,
Class of 1979

Christopher Bridges graduated from the University of London in 1988 and was called to the Bar of England and Wales by the Honourable Society of the Inner Temple in 1989 after sitting for the Bar Finals where he won a Book Prize for Best Overseas Student in General Paper 1. He was admitted as an Advocate and Solicitor to The Supreme Court, Republic of Singapore on 6 June 1990. He is a Notary Public and a Commissioner for Oaths.

Christopher has over 25 years' experience as a litigator and practises General Litigation. His field of practice as a General Litigator is wide and varied. He is accredited on the List of Leading Counsel maintained by the High Court of Singapore which appoints on behalf of the State, senior criminal practitioners who are assisted by an assistant Counsel from a similar List of Assisting Counsel to represent a Defendant facing the Death Penalty and whose fees are paid for by the High Court.

He has served on various sub-committees in the Law Society of Singapore and has been recognized

Christopher pictured on the right with a German colleague.

by the Criminal Legal Aid Scheme for his contributions to this Scheme in 1997. On 19 October 2011, he was awarded the "Minister of Law Appreciation Award" for his services to the Legal Aid Bureau of the Ministry of Law. He has a strong conviction in giving our wayward youth a second chance so Christopher works tirelessly to rehabilitate them. He is also a gazetted volunteer Probation Officer.

"The best years of my life were the years I spent in SJI. I really enjoyed myself there. I remember Bro. Dennis Watts, I think he is gone already. He once came up to me and said, 'You know Chris, your dialect group is English and you have an English sounding name. Don't you think it is humiliating if you only get 51 marks in the exam?' That really woke me up and I took up the hobby of reading. Till today, I still remember the first three books I read: *War of the Running Dogs* and *Sinister Twilight* by Noel Barber, and *The Jungle Is Neutral* by F. Spencer Chapman. I developed a love for reading and after that my grades improved."

"I looked forward to going to school everyday. Hamish Brown, the former Radio DJ, used to sit next to me. Everyday we used to go to school and crack jokes and what not. There was this guy, Patrick Mosely from New Zealand. He did not know what a chilli was. In art class, we had to paint paintings with fruits and vegetables. We told him a chilli is as sweet as an apple. He literally bit half of the chilli. These are the kinds of pranks we used to play."

"We also had teachers like Wong Fatt How and Francis Loh who we referred to as "F" low. He was the discipline master. His son was in the same batch as us. We are still good friends, we still keep in touch. When we meet each other, we are back to being 16-year-old boys. We act like 16-year-old boys again

> *The best years of my life were the years I spent in SJI.*

which is good because it brings us back down to earth."

"SJI has made me a much better person; more optimistic and more down to earth. SJI has a value system in that we don't judge people and everyone is equal. It also incorporates a system of charity work. SJI taught me to give back to society. I always believe in second chances. I am a probation officer because I want to give guidance to the youngsters. I was once a youngster and there would be certain periods I would rebel as well. I saw the errors of my ways and I changed. Youngsters may be rascals but that does not mean they are not good people. You should always give them a chance."

SJI taught me to give back to society. I always believe in second chances.

GILBERT LAU KWANG FATT

Senior Consultant Forensic Pathologist and Director of Professional Practice at the Forensic Medicine Division of Health Sciences Authority, Class of 1976

After obtaining his MBBS (SG), MRCPath (UK), DMJ (Lon), FAMS and FRCPath, Associate Professor Gilbert Lau Kwang Fatt began his medical practice as a forensic pathologist and is now the Director of Professional Practice at the Forensic Medicine Division of Health Sciences Authority (HSA). Gilbert's career is not for the faint-hearted. He deals with corpses and hypothesises the possible cause of death based on evidence from the corpse. He has been entrusted with some of the most infamous cases in the region, including the Kovan Double Murders of 2013. Gilbert holds memberships within various HSA boards and editorial boards, and chairs the Forensic Sub-committee in the Specialist Training Committee in Pathology. Gilbert is a Clinical Professor and Posting Director for forensic medicine at Yong Yoo Lin School of Medicine-NUS, who has also published many academic papers and is frequently invited to lecture overseas. For his service, Gilbert was awarded the Public Service Medal and Public Administration Medal (Bronze) during the National Day Awards of 2005 and 2013, respectively.

Gilbert expresses that he has no regrets attending SJI, despite a lack of air-conditioning. Gilbert fondly remembers his teachers' idiosyncrasies, his friends and the experiences shared. He still maintains these friendships, and expresses admiration for the perseverance and passion of a friend of his who was, originally, a PE teacher at SJI, but subsequently obtained a PhD in biokinetics and is, currently, a senior lecturer at NTU.

Apart from being the Class Monitor in Secondary 4, Gilbert was involved in the Society of St. Vincent De Paul. Interacting with peers of different backgrounds taught him to never discriminate and he hopes that this inclusivity in SJI will never be lost. As it was for him, Gilbert wishes that SJI will remain a "safe haven" for future Josephians in times of uncertainty, nurturing them in all aspects of life.

"Life is more than just a career. Each of us must discover and pursue our passions in life. We must take time to do this and not be swayed by thoughts of quick success."

> *Life is more than just a career. Each of us must discover and pursue our passions in life. We must take time to do this and not be swayed by thoughts of quick success.*

Tan Siong Thye

*High Court Judge of the Supreme Court
of the Republic of Singapore,
Class of 1970*

Tan Siong Thye has an illustrious legal career since graduating from the National University of Singapore. He is now a High Court Judge of the Supreme Court. Prior to this appointment he was the first Deputy Attorney-General of Singapore. His previous appointments include the Chief District Judge of the Subordinate Courts (now known as the State Courts) and the Director of the Commercial Affairs Department.

He had served National Service for 29 years and was also a volunteer in the Singapore Armed Forces (SAF). He was a field commander with the rank of a Colonel before he retired from the SAF. He was also a member of the Military Court of Appeal for 13 years.

For his sterling service to the nation, he was awarded several National Awards including NS Man of the Year 1997 and the Public Administration (Gold) (Bar) 2011.

Despite his success and stature, Mr Tan remains humble and firmly remembers his roots. He was a school prefect and stays true to his Alma Mater, SJI,

For Mr Tan Siong Thye, SJI helped intensify his sense of servant leadership.

crediting the school for turning him into the man he is today. He vividly recalls the old Bras Basah campus (currently Singapore Art Museum) where SJI once stood in the late 1960s.

One of the most important memories that Mr Tan still holds dear to date is his scouting experience. As part of the now defunct 2103 Hippo Scout Troop, he fondly remembers the adventures of hiking, trekking, camping and building large wooden shelters. Along with the other scouts, he would cut bamboos and make them into all kinds of household items such as benches, tables and gateways for the purpose of camping. He also took part in scouting competitions such as tent pitching and fireman's ladder. Mr Tan acknowledges the prodigious contributions of the Hippo scout alumni, such as Mr Foo Chi Kai, Mr Sim Hock Thye and others, to the scout movement in SJI. They were hugely passionate and totally committed to scouting. In fact, they selflessly contributed their time, effort and money to impart their experience and skill of scouting to the younger generation of scouts.

Every Christmas Mr Tan meets up with the scout alumni at the home of Mr Michael Sng, another staunch and completely devoted Hippo alumni. They reminisce about the good old times in SJI. It is apparent that he has forged strong bonds with the Josephians during his time in SJI.

Mr Tan also developed servant leadership during his scouting days. Mr Tan elaborated, "If you are in the position of authority, you are a little blessed so you must in turn help others especially the less fortunate. I look after everyone in every organisation that I am in." This has become a part of his DNA.

Mr Tan was also part of the SJI loyalist — a group of loyal students who remained in SJI for the pre-U education (currently known as JC) after graduating

> **If you are in the position of authority, you are a little blessed so you must in turn help others especially the less fortunate.**

in Secondary 4. These students chose to stay on in SJI even when they were offered a place in National Junior College, the only Junior College in Singapore at that time. Other notable alumni of this batch would be Deputy Prime Minister Teo Chee Hean, and former Minister for Foreign Affairs George Yeo.

Mr Tan is thankful and grateful to the principals and teachers of SJI. He says:

"I am deeply grateful to the Principals of SJI for their sterling and exemplary leadership as well as to the teachers, especially Mr Benedict Oei, for their dedication and huge devotion to the interests of the students. They had imbued in me the right values and morals which define my character. These have been instrumental in my decision-making through-out my adulthood and more importantly in the discharge of my official duties."

Mr Tan's parting advice to the students is:

> **Life is like a never-ending roller coaster ride with its ups and downs so you must overcome failure quickly and bounce back with a vengeance to succeed.**

"Learn to stand firmly on your own two feet. One day you'll have your own family and your parents won't be there forever to help you. You must be ready to take on the world and adversities. Be a unique individual who possesses creative ideation but always rooted in humility, integrity and a strong sense of fairness. Life is like a never-ending roller coaster ride with its ups and downs so you must overcome failure quickly and bounce back with a vengeance to succeed. There is much to learn from failure so you should embrace failure and move on with life. Always remember SJI's motto — 'Ora et labora.'"

For
MEDICINE

Damian (holding a hymnal) at mass with 200 A Call to Share (ACTS) participants at morning mass in Battambang, Cambodia.

Damian Png

Senior Consultant Urologist &
Chairman of "A Call to Share",
Class of 1978

After graduating from SJI in 1978, Dr Damian Png Jin Chye pursued a speciality in urology in National University of Singapore (NUS), the United Kingdom and Germany. Damian is an accredited renal transplant surgeon and has served as Assistant Professor at NUS for 13 years. He is now in private practice in Mount Elizabeth and Parkway East Hospital.

"The most exciting time in SJI was the football games with RI. Whenever there was a big match, the whole school would cross over to the field opposite, where we did a lot of sports and football. There was also a sports shop opposite Waterloo Street and those were the days when one football was enough entertainment."

"There you also had your sarabat drinks stall, your rojak, your soup kambing and more. We did not have much money, so we would 'maximise' our order by asking for a lot of side vegetables like onions and cucumbers."

"My friends and I were taught by Brother Kevin Byrne before he became principal. We were quite

> **"**
> *Whenever there was a big match, the whole school would cross over to the field opposite, where we did a lot of sports and football.*
> **"**

naughty, and he was a tough but fair and a good teacher. Nowadays, I still keep in touch with a lot of ex Josephians including three of my boys who were also from SJI. The friends you end up keeping in the long term are the ones you grew up with in Secondary School, your formative years."

"Most of my SJI friends ended up in the NUS medical school. My mother wanted me to be a doctor, but I had resisted in the early years; you do the opposite of what your parents tell you to do. It was only after my A-Levels when I sat down and thought about what I wanted to do with my life, that medicine seemed to be the perfect fit. I like to help people, and medicine was one profession where work and personal beliefs could be easily aligned."

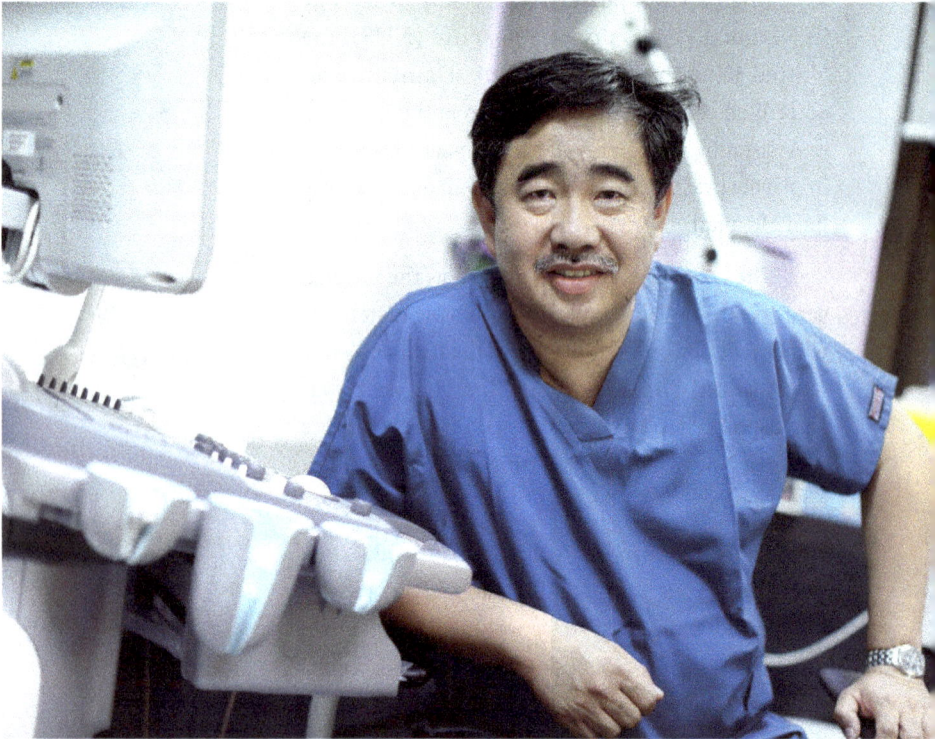

Damian says being a doctor allows him to align his work and personal values.

"I think my Catholic faith led me to become a doctor. Being a doctor allows me to exercise my mission and social duties as a Catholic and help others along this journey of faith. It is one of those things that I enjoy and feel a sense of peace and joy in, two things which a lot of people seek. So, if you asked me whether I would do medicine again, I would."

Damian is also actively involved in community service: "I have been leading outreach teams to Cambodia in ACTS, which stands for 'A Call to Share'. We help with education and healthcare needs in poorer regional communities."

"We believe that the wealth of the world belongs to everyone. The more you are given, the more responsibilities you have. I have been blessed enough as a doctor with a close family and I want to redistribute my blessings. In ACTS, we share whatever that we have — experiences of love, compassion or forgiveness, and the joy of giving. When you give your ice-cream to a kid, you see the joy on their faces which is worth far more than that ice-cream."

"I only started to appreciate SJI a lot more after I left. SJI has a certain Catholic spirit which is very precious — for example Friday mass, morning prayers, confessions and penitential service etc. These are things — values you want to keep and treasure — which are special to SJI, that you cannot replace with education and grades. We always go through problems together, and I think that is the bond and the spirit that we should always nurture."

> *We believe that the wealth of the world belongs to everyone. The more you are given, the more responsibilities you have.*

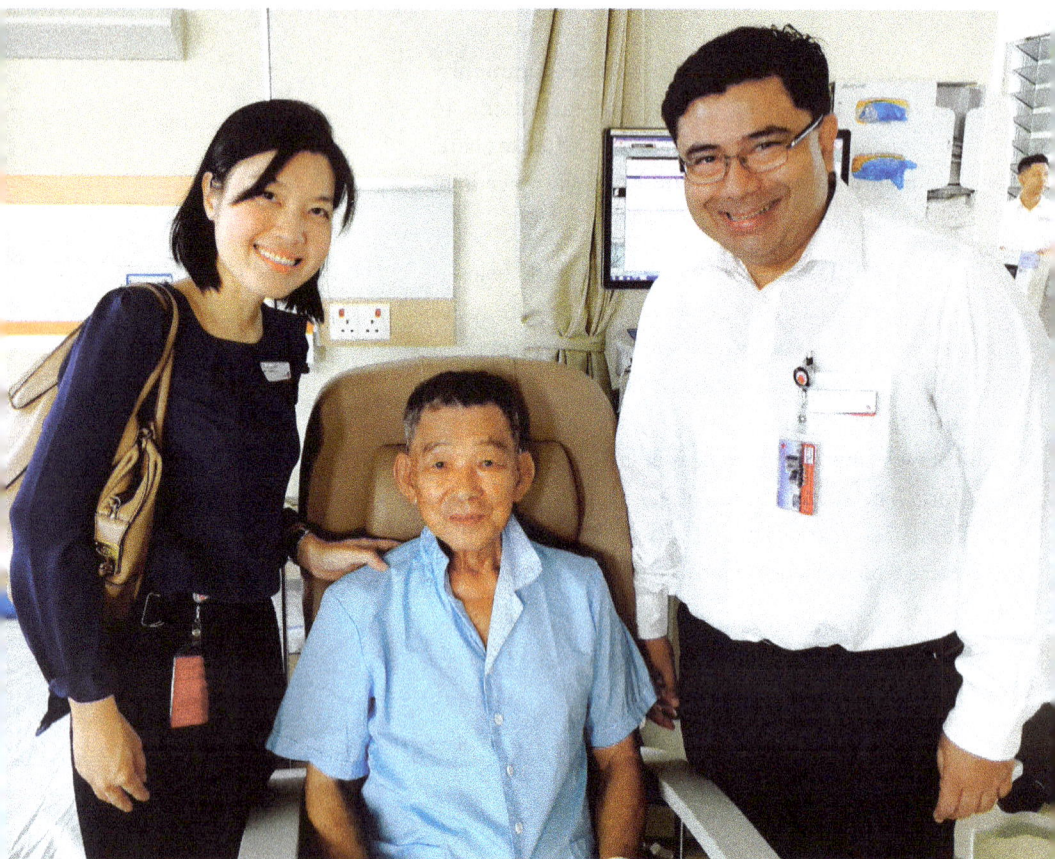

Euan on the right with a cochlear implant patient.

EUAN MURUGASU

*Head and Senior Consultant of the
Department of ENT — Head and Neck Surgery
at Jurong Health Services,
Class of 1978*

D r Euan Murugasu excelled academically,
receiving the Frank James Trophy (SJI) and the
Ee Peng Liang Gold Medal (CJC) before receiving
the President's Scholarship in 1981 to pursue
medicine. Euan completed his specialisation in
otorhinolaryngology with an MBBS, two FRCS, an
FAMS, and a Ph.D. (Sussex), where his thesis won
him several prestigious awards. Euan is now Head
of the Department of ENT — Head and Neck Surgery
at Jurong Health and has built a new ENT Department.
Additionally, Euan is passionate about education and
volunteerism. Amongst his various appointments,
Euan serves as a Board Member of the Canossian
School for the Hearing Impaired and Chairman of
CDAC@Punggol.

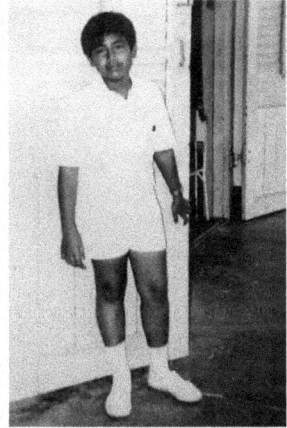

Euan in SJI, 1975.

"SJI was where you made friends for life. My
class, the Class of '78 and even the prefects still plan
get-togethers. When we found out one of our fellow
prefects had advanced lung cancer, we deliberately
organised meals just to get together and cheer him
up. I think it is unusual that after 40 years, we still
choose to keep in touch, meet up, and support each
other."

66

*SJI was where you
made friends for life.*

99

Euan with the 1978 Prefects.

> **The teachers had a wonderful spirit of forgiveness. Their dedication and sheer delight of having them around was one of the great treasures of SJI.**

"To this day, I am still in touch with my teachers like Ms Charlotte Collars and Mrs Joan Fong. I also kept in touch with the late Bro. Kevin Byrne even after he retired and went back to Ireland. Brother Kevin inspired us to try and do the best we can. He would always encourage us and be there for us. He was a very soft-spoken and mild-mannered man, but he had very firm beliefs and values, which I think he passed on not only to us, but to a few generations of Josephians."

"I think it shocked him to get us as his first form class when he came to Singapore from Penang. In Sec 4 Science 6, we were very bright but mischievous kids, and we took delight in devising games and tricks to torture our teachers. Bro. Kevin was our literature teacher and we hated our book 'Brighton Rock'. Someone would always answer Brother Kevin's questions but in truth, everyone read only one section. The teachers had a wonderful spirit of forgiveness. Their dedication and sheer delight of having them around was one of the great treasures of SJI."

"I was in Scouts, the LDDS and the school choir. I learnt how to cook in the Scouts, and won my patrol a prize for cooking a chicken underground at Sarimbun. I had the chance to represent SJI at the Singapore Youth Festival and several oratorical and debate events. I am quite introverted, but I was forced to embrace public speaking by my teachers, not something that I instinctively enjoyed going through. My teacher also made it his mission in life to make sure that I spoke proper Mandarin. His efforts paid off and to this day, I cannot believe that we managed to win the first place at the Sin Chew Jit Poh National Chinese Oratorical Competition."

"If I did not do medicine, I would have done something

Euan with the 1978 Prefects at a recent dinner.

totally out of the box like Politics, Philosophy and Economics. At that time, the government was trying very hard to offer scholarships to move us away from the sciences like medicine and engineering. I am quite a rebel at heart, so I tend to go against these kinds of decisions that people force on you. Nowadays I see patients almost every day and operate at least once a week. My own interest is in the ear and we offer cochlear implants to help profondly deaf persons to hear again. I raise donations to help people who cannot afford this technology. It is quite interesting and there are always new surprises, but the greatest reward is still a grateful patient."

"SJI's school motto is 'Ora et Labora'. At the risk of being evicted from the Old Boys' Association, I added my own phrase — Ora et Labora, Laboris Gloria Ludi (study hard, play hard and pray hard). You have to study and work hard, but know how to relax, let your hair down and enjoy. I think that as a Christian Brother School, we should not forget to pray to give thanks and to pray when you need help. When good times come, give thanks; when bad times hit, seek God and his comfort. I think the SJI experience really teaches these beliefs."

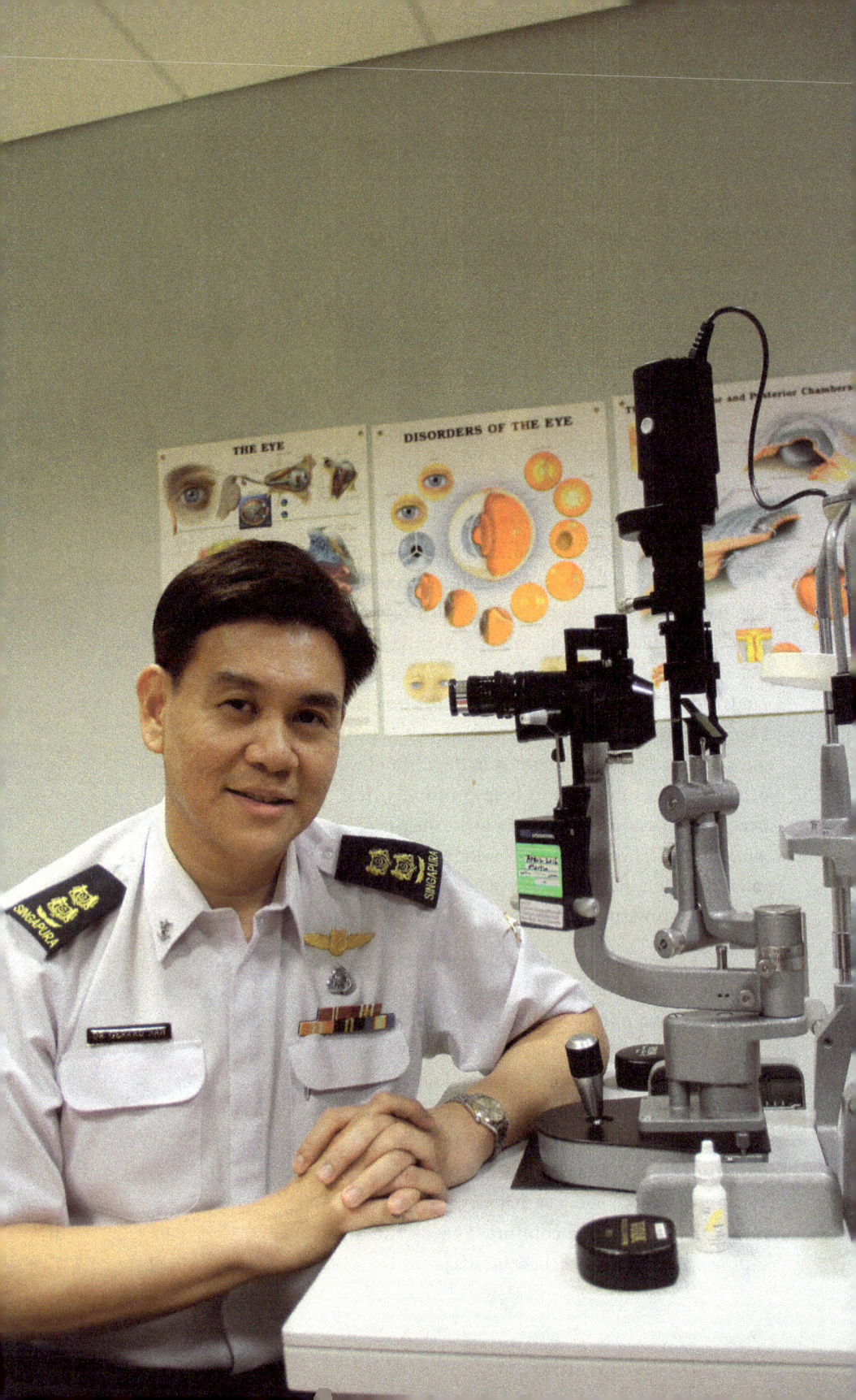

GERARD NAH

Founder of the SAF Vision Performance Centre,
Director, W Eye Clinic,
Class of 1984

D r Gerard Nah is a Senior Eye Surgeon trained in the sub-specialty of Cornea, Refractive Surgery and External Diseases. A medical graduate from the University of Aberdeen in the UK, he underwent and completed his training as an eye surgeon in Singapore under the Singapore Armed Forces Post-graduate Scholarship (Medical) programme. He then went on to train as a clinical fellow at the University of British Columbia. He is a Fellow of the Royal College of Surgeons of Edinburgh and holds a Masters of Medicine in Ophthalmology from NUS. He also received his Diploma in Aviation Medicine from the Royal College of Physicians of London and was awarded the Barbara Harrison Memorial Prize for best overseas student in his course. Gerard is a leading figure in aviation medicine and military ophthalmology.

The proud serviceman of 20 years in the Republic of Singapore Air Force who founded the SAF Vision Performance Centre, was the head of the RSAF Aeromedical Centre and served as the

Left: Gerard is a third generation Josephian.

international-chair of the Annual International Military Refractive Surgery Symposium from 2007 to 2013. For his service to the nation, he was awarded the Commendation Medal (Military) at the 2011 National Day Awards. After 20 years of service, Gerard remains an active reservist in the SAF as Senior Lieutenant Colonel and Eye Specialist. He has worked with the SAF to volunteer for missions overseas to provide free eye surgery for the poor. Gerard is now the Medical Director at W Eye Clinic.

A third-generation Josephian, SJI played a quintessential role in shaping Gerard's character. Struggling with Chinese when studying for his PSLE, Gerard had to appeal into SJI, which taught him to never take anything for granted. He became a diligent student who found his place in several clubs and societies. SJI has a particularly special place in his heart because, it was in the chapel of SJI that Gerard was baptised, while being a member of the Legion of Mary.

SJI has always been a very big part of Gerard's life. He is the current President of the SJI Old Boys Association (SJIOBA), where he has been inspired by his many interactions with older and younger Josephians. Gerard feels strongly that the SJIOBA is an important part of keeping the SJI traditions alive.

Gerard actively partakes in various ministries such as the Infant Baptism Ministry and the Roman Catholic Prison Ministry. Prisoners are an often-forgotten group in society, and he finds giving religious counselling to prisoners one of the most fulfilling things he has ever done. He echoes the Josephian belief that we are called to serve, and SJI taught him to find a meaningful life in serving a higher cause rather than fulfilling one's selfish desires.

66

SJI has a particularly special place in his heart because, it was in the chapel of SJI that Gerard was baptised, while being a member of the Legion of Mary.

99

"Everybody is called to serve in their own way. Not all of us can do great things, but through the small things we do with great love, we can contribute greatly to the community. When you serve, serve like the parable of the widow's mite — even if you do not have much to begin with, serve with all that you have in all sincerity and purity of intention."

"At the end of your life, you are going to look back and ask yourself what this life was for. Was it for yourself? Was it for something better, something greater? Something that would allow you to say, 'this was a good life.'"

"It was not a life about me — it was a life where I have made a difference in this world. I think that is an important part of the SJI upbringing."

> *Everybody is called to serve in their own way. Not all of us can do great things, but through the small things we do with great love, we can contribute greatly to the community.*

Eng Eong believes that we are here to help others, and we are here to contribute to others.
[© Duke-NUS]

Ooi Eng Eong

*Professor and Deputy Director of
Emerging Infectious Diseases Programme
at Duke-NUS Medical School,
Class of 1984*

D
r Ooi Eng Eong holds a BMBS, a Ph.D. in Molecular Epidemiology, an M.Sc. and DLSHTM in Medicinal Microbiology and an FRCPath in Virology. A brilliant researcher, Eng Eong has held various positions with the DSO National Laboratories, the National Environment Agency and the Ministry of Health. For his notable research contributions to the war against dengue, he received the National Medical Research Council Clinician-Scientist Award (Senior Investigator Category) and a patent.

"Being in SJI was one of the best times of my life. I do not remember ever dreading school. I would start the day at 7.30 a.m. and after school, we would have lunch together; and I still keep in touch with the same group today. Afterwards, the two of us in Track and Field would train at the National Stadium till 6 p.m. It was fun spending a whole day with my friends."

66

*Being in SJI was one
of the best times of
my life... It was fun
spending a whole
day with my friends.*

99

"Back then, SJI was very united and the school did not make distinctions between students. So long as the students wanted to be there, there was no reason why the school would not take them. The whole spirit of education, the De La Salle background — that there was a well-rounded education for everyone who wanted it, was very inspiring."

"I remember first wanting to be a doctor in Secondary 2. I really enjoyed science, especially Chemistry and Biology. Medicine was the profession that everyone aspired towards, and I certainly did not expect myself to end up as a researcher when I went to medical school. But while I was working as a doctor, I felt more frustrated than rewarded. In the way medicine works today, we patch a problem but do not actually solve it. We cannot cure some diseases because we do not understand the mechanisms behind them. That is why I switched to research."

> *If you can contribute to society, that by itself is more rewarding than any riches. If what we are doing leads to a dengue vaccine, I would retire happily.*

"Becoming rich never once crossed my mind. If I wanted to become rich, I would never have become a researcher. I very much enjoy my current expertise and I think it is one of those rare jobs that you can describe as 'fun'. Research is largely curiosity driven, so to be successful you have to have an interest which inspires you to dig for knowledge. But there is also the practical side. There must be a balance between wanting to pursue something because it is interesting, and asking yourself if this would lead to an outcome that would benefit mankind."

"SJI taught me that you are not here for yourself; you are here to help others, and you are here to contribute to others. If you can contribute to society, that by itself is more rewarding than any riches. If what we are doing leads to a dengue vaccine, I would retire happily."

"I think most Josephians would go ahead and do what we think is right, whether it is easy or not. Similarly, faith is a guiding light in research. For example, where do you draw the line with gene editing? There is this grey area today which may be clear-cut in 10 years' time, but until then your faith and the principles you choose to live by will be your guiding light on how to deal with things."

"Being in SJI is one of my most cherished memories. I had a lot of fun and though it has changed quite a lot, I still go back to Bras Basah to show my school to my kids and friends."

"If I could, I would live it all over again."

66
Faith is a guiding light in research.
99

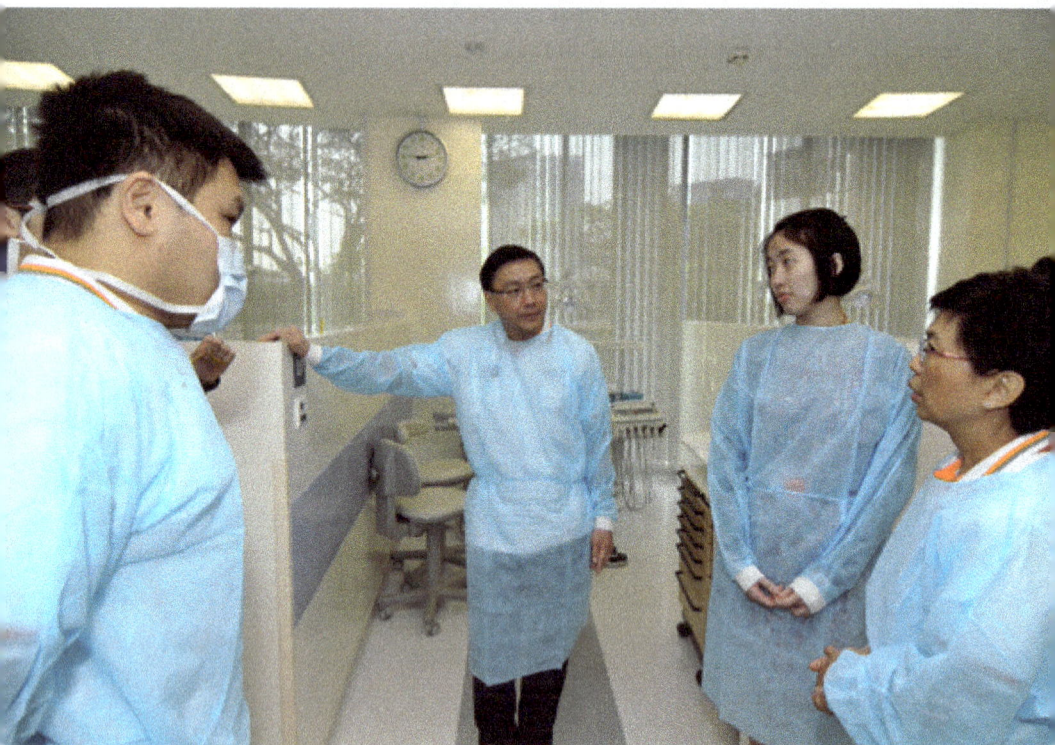

Patrick interacting with alumni and students and helping out at the Faculty of Dentistry health screening.

PATRICK TSENG

Chief Dental Officer of the Ministry of Health,
Class of 1976

Professor Patrick Tseng Seng Kwong received his Bachelor of Dental Surgery degree in 1985 from National University of Singapore (NUS) and a Master of Science in Endodontics with Distinction in 1990 from the University of London. The awardee of the Fellow of the International College of Dentists (1997) and Fellow of the Academy of Dentists International (1998) is also a Founder Member of the Society of Endodontists in Singapore and holds many appointments such as Registrar of the Singapore Dental Council, Chairman of the Specialist Accreditation Board and Chairman of the Oral Health Therapists Accreditation Committee. Serving over 30 years in National University Hospital (NUH), Patrick is a sought-after international speaker and Clinical Associate Professor in the NUS Dental Faculty and the Chief Dental Officer at the Ministry of Health.

> **His scout name was 'Pelandok'.**

"I am the second of three generations of Josephians. My father, a neurosurgeon, passed away when I was only two. My mother would later remarry my father's brother, Uncle James, an SJI old boy too. His scout name was 'Pelandok'; who founded the

Patrick (second from right) with the 4 Science 7 Swim Team.

scout group in SJI post-war."

"We did a lot of things in SJI. Everyone in Lower Secondary had to attend technical workshops at McNair Road and every week, we would walk to Fort Canning for lunch before class started. We also enjoyed sports and CCA. You could do whatever type or number of CCAs you wanted to, and then try to cope with your studies. Rather than the CCAs, I thought the academic part was the more stressful."

"I was very active in Scouts. I remember the friendships made hiking through the wilderness with only a map and compass. We had fun camping and experiencing new things at Sarimbun. We didn't have showers, we cooked rice in bamboo and once, we had to cook a live chicken. Being our first time, the guy holding the chicken, as it was cut, let it go, and it ran around with its head off with blood flying all over before we caught it and baked it in clay. Its feathers came off with the clay and it was so tender. It was interesting what you could do with things from nature."

"I was also very interested in sports. I represented SJI in athletics, badminton and tennis, and I was the soccer captain in Secondary 4. We would play soccer all the time before school started and come to class all sweaty. Our soccer team was strong and we came in third for the nationals."

"Soccer teaches you teamwork, and as in life, nothing can be achieved as an individual. You are completely dependent on others as they are on you. Even now I learn from my graduate students as they learn from me — the probing questions they ask, the cases they bring in, their new views on treatment plans. Nobody can survive on their own and everyone is dependent on each other."

Patrick (standing third from left) with the Pelandok Football Team.

"I love my job. Even as an undergraduate, I enjoyed what I was doing. I would not call myself a very religious person. There is some luck involved in finding something you enjoy doing but as a Catholic, I believe that God led the way. The start-up page on my laptop is the Jesuit Prayer Ministry's website and the first thing I do every morning is read the gospel and reflect."

"Always do unto others as you would have them do unto you. I constantly put myself in the shoes of my students, my staff and most importantly, my patients, and reflect on how as that person I would want to be treated."

Philip recalls that SJI was an unusual place with teachers who would allow you to do what seems impossible nowadays.

Philip Choo

Chief Executive Officer of the National Health Group, Class of 1974

Professor Philip Choo holds a slew of prestigious medical qualifications from the Royal Colleges of Physicians from London, Glasgow and Edinburgh, and was awarded an HMDP Fellowship for Geriatric Medicine. He is now a Senior Consultant in Geriatric Medicine at Tan Tock Seng Hospital, as well as the Group Chief Executive Officer of the National Healthcare Group. For his contributions to the nation, Philip was awarded the Public Service Star Award (BBM) and the Public Administration Medal (Silver) during the National Day Awards in 2003 and 2011, respectively.

Philip's unusual childhood, where he and his siblings were sent to Singapore following the May 13 riots in Malaysia in 1969, shaped his ability to think and fend for himself.

He recounts, "My three siblings and I lived on our own in Singapore as our parents were in Malaysia. We had to do almost everything ourselves, from paying the rent to keeping the flat in running order. Each of us was responsible for different aspects of running a home."

> *We had to do almost everything ourselves, from paying the rent to keeping the flat in running order.*

Philip Choo at a hospital event.

"I was in charge of finance, and I had to bank in the monthly cheque from my parents, disburse the money to each sibling accordingly, while ensuring we all kept within our allotted budget. We learnt how to work together as well as take accountability in our respective roles early in life. This taught me more than any school appointment I held," he states. Philip was class monitor and prefect in primary school.

As Philip's grandfather believed in the value of an English education, he ended up sending all his sons and daughters to mission schools. Hence Philip's father did likewise and Philip and his brother ended up in SJI.

Philip says, "My father, uncles and cousins were all from SJI. SJI was quite fun in those days. It was an unusual place where teachers would allow you to do what seems impossible nowadays." Teachers were then more open to students taking the initiative and running enterprises on their own.

"Within the Careers Club, students could operate without supervision an old-fashioned printing press with stencils, printing and distributing researched articles on various career opportunities and their requisite university qualifications. We could actually run things our way, gaining hands-on experience as we went," he adds.

Those formative years in SJI helped Philip develop an independent spirit and his own way of thinking which was critical in his choice of geriatric medicine.

"I was the first doctor to be trained in geriatric medicine in those days. Some of my contemporaries and seniors thought I was absolutely crazy to venture into an unknown discipline. But once I made up my mind, I thought it was important to see it through. And so off to Glasgow I went."

During his time in Glasgow, Philip learned more than just geriatric medicine.

"My mentor taught me a lot of important things in life beyond medicine. He told me you will never get anywhere in life unless you always add value. You must also be likeable, trustworthy, helpful, and generous."

One of the defining moments in Philip's career was when SARS (Severe acute respiratory syndrome) hit Singapore in 2003. He was, at the time, the clinical leader in Tan Tock Seng Hospital and needed to manage the crisis when it struck.

"When chaos hits, a leader must rise above personal fear and take the lead firmly by willing to expose himself to the same risks as his team members. Only then will order be established as people follow your lead with no hesitation."

Since graduation in 1982, Philip has worked in the public sector and loves his job immensely.

> *When chaos hits, a leader must rise above personal fear and take the lead firmly by willing to expose himself to the same risks as his team members.*

"Understand that you are here to serve. Many people enter medicine see it only as a respectable money-maker, and they are not prepared to give and serve. You are married to the hospital for the first decade after you graduate. This may sound demanding but it can also be one of the most rewarding careers ever. Work life can be filled with challenges, but it is also filled with instant gratification when patients and their families show appreciation."

Philip's job scope has changed tremendously over the years as he rose through the ranks.

"I started my career as a clinician but I am now essentially an administrator. Many doctors shy away from becoming administrators because they no longer see patients much which is the reason they entered medicine in the first place. What they fail to see is that working as an administrator you can have a bigger impact on healthcare."

When asked if he has any final words, he shared this story with us:

"One of the most valuable lessons I have learnt from a previous boss is to always do things for the right reasons without expecting anyone to applaud you for it. Instead, expect brickbats and criticism."

"I remember when I submitted a letter of resignation, unhappy over a complaint from a patient, only to have it thrown back in my face with these words from my boss: 'Do not expect recognition or reward for doing the right thing. In fact, expect criticism for you cannot please everyone, all of the time. This is the nature of public service. As long as your peers respect your decisions, and you know you acted with integrity, that is all that matters. If you can accept this, stay, if not, leave, but I think you can.' He wasn't wrong," laughs Philip.

> 66
> *Do not expect recognition or reward for doing the right thing.*
> 99

TERESA LEE

Adjunct Associate Professor, Faculty of Dentistry at National University of Singapore, Class of 1957

D r Teresa Lee was, until recently, one of the rarest types of students from SJI — a female student. Dr Lee, a dentist, has had an illustrious career during which time she was awarded a number of scholarships and academic prizes including the Colombo Plan to pursue a post graduate course in Dental Public Health at the University of Sydney in 1970, a World Health Organisation Fellowship to study Dental Services and Health Education in New Zealand in 1972 and a University Book Prize at her final exams. She has been involved in Dentistry for more than five decades, spanning practice, academia and administration. During this time she actively led and chaired many local and international committees including that for Singapore's Ministry of Health as well as being the first President of the Singapore Dental Foundation.

For her tireless service, Teresa was awarded the Public Administration Medal at the 1985 National Day Awards and has been listed on the Singapore Dental Association's Roll of Honour (2001).

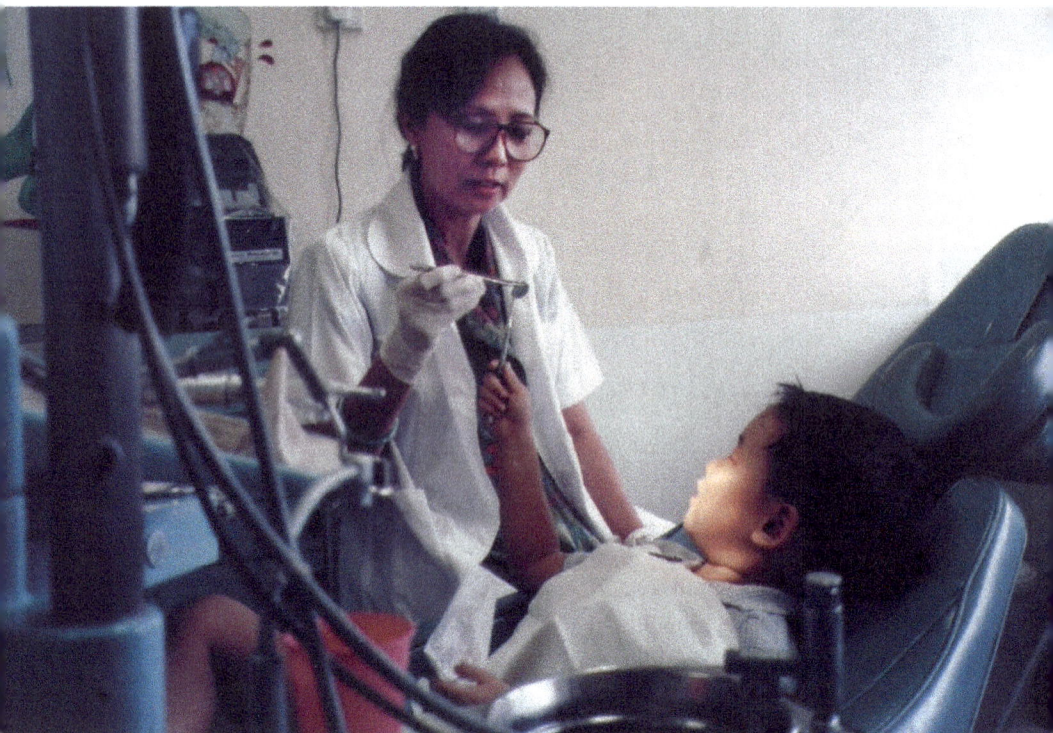

Teresa recalls that the SJI boys were rather cheeky but always helpful.

Since 2003, Teresa has been teaching as an Adjunct Associate Professor of the Faculty of Dentistry at the National University of Singapore.

"Back in those days, there was no Pre- University course for science in CHIJ Victoria Street. Six of us from CHIJ, who were passionate about science and had every intention to pursue science, joined the boys of SJI at Bras Basah Road. One female student left shortly after commencing the course. However, the remaining five of us persevered and completed our Higher School certificate examination at SJI, which enabled us to gain entrance to the University of Singapore. Of us five, three were accepted to read Science, one to Medicine and I to Dentistry. It was my aunt, then a dental nurse, who inspired me to pursue Dentistry as a career, however unusual it was then."

"In the early days the boys in SJI were rather

cheeky but surprisingly very self-conscious. I recall that at our very first science lesson, us girls got together and occupied the front row of seats in class. Subsequently, not to be outdone, the boys moved to occupy the front rows of seats and started to behave in a loud and intrusive manner and we girls decided that we would only obtain peace and quiet if we stayed far away from these posturing SJI boys and we ended up right at the back of the class. Nevertheless at no time were these SJI boys of yore less than gentlemen. They were always ready to help in true Lasallian spirit. When asked, they never hesitated to help, especially during science experiments. We forged such a relationship that, to this day, I still meet up with some of them socially."

"I have had a truly fulfilling career. In fact, I would say I am one of the few dentists who has had the opportunity to work in the various dental services in the Dental Division of the Ministry of Health excepting the polyclinics. Following the end of my first year at the Singapore General Hospital, I was tasked to teach in the Dental Nurses Training School, which I enjoyed very much. Then I was blessed to be awarded a Colombo Plan Scholarship to undertake postgraduate studies and this gave me more responsibilities and choices. When the Dental Health Education Unit was mooted in the Dental Division, I asked to be posted there as I felt that the promotion of good dental health to the population at large was critical. My final posting in the Ministry was to the School Dental Service to assist the then Director and I assumed the role of Director for School Dental Service upon his retirement. This role later broadened to include the training of dental auxiliaries. I truly enjoyed my appointment as the Director, School Dental Service, Training and Health Education. I had excellent staff who were cohesive and worked collectively as a team."

> *At no time were these SJI boys of yore less than gentlemen. They were always ready to help in true Lasallian spirit.*

Following her retirement from the Ministry of Health, Teresa continued her lifelong passion for Dentistry by joining the National University as an academic where she is an Adjunct Associate Professor.

Teresa remains a steadfast believer in the importance of charity work and giving back to society. "We must always show empathy towards the less fortunate, and those in need." To inculcate this belief in others, Teresa arranged for her students to visit homes for the elderly so that they too can have some understanding of the challenges faced by the elderly and less fortunate.

"I have seen many elderly people who are so weak that they have difficulty even holding a toothbrush and have no one to help with regular tooth brushing. Some of them are in desperate need of dentures so they can chew solid food. It is sad to see these elderly left to fend for themselves."

"My upbringing and education in both a convent and a Lasallian School instilled in me a set of values about life and the lives we lead. I was repeatedly taught that it is not only the attendance of mass, even on a daily basis. It is about kindness, consideration and generosity of spirit."

Teresa has not forgotten the blessings and gifts that she has received. She continues to actively involve herself in charity work, from the simple act of participation in jumble sales at her parish Church to free dental care to the needy overseas. "I want to share my favourite quote from Mother Teresa that I strive to achieve daily: 'What good you do today, is forgotten tomorrow, but do good anyway.' We must always endeavour to do good without consideration or seeking recognition or praise. It will lead us right and to the light."

> 66
> *We must always endeavour to do good without consideration or seeking recognition or praise. It will lead us right and to the light.*
> 99

THOMAS LEW WING KIT

———— ⟨♠⟩ ————

Chairman, Medical Board,
Tan Tock Seng Hospital,
Class of 1977

Associate Professor Thomas Lew Wing Kit is a dual specialist in Anaesthesiology and Intensive Care Medicine, with an MBBS, an MMed (Anaes), an EDIC and an FAMS under his belt. He attended the Berkeley-NTU Advanced Management and the Social Leadership Singapore Programmes, which nurtured his interests in Leadership, Management and Social Services. He pioneered the development of neurological intensive care services at Tan Tock Seng Hospital and the National Neuroscience Institute (NNI) in the 1990s. He was President of the Singapore Society of Anaesthesiologists, and a Founding Member of the Society of Intensive Care Medicine (Singapore) and the Asian Society of Neuroanaesthesia and Critical Care. Thomas also teaches as a Clinical Associate Professor at NUS Yong Yoo Lin School of Medicine and Adjunct Associate Professor at the Lee Kong Chian School of Medicine, NTU. He has chaired Tan Tock Seng Hospital's Clinical Board since 2011, overseeing its core clinical mission. He is married to Dr Cheong Lai Leng, a Dermatologist, and they have two sons, Simon and Adrian.

"School was a nice place to hang out with friends," recalls Thomas who still keeps in contact with many of his friends from SJI. He fondly remembers playing sports with his friends and the many camping adventures to places like Coney Island, Pulau Tekong and Pulau Ubin. Thomas was a member of NCC Air where he learnt the leadership, discipline and determination required in his course of life. Such opportunities helped train him for his tenure as a senior prefect in his Upper Secondary years, which Thomas felt was a privilege.

Thomas heard a calling to serve for a higher purpose. Wanting to do something worthwhile, Thomas picked medicine not for its paycheque but for its opportunities to help others. In addition to enjoying research, Thomas is cheered when his patients who have entrusted their lives to him recover, motivating him to constantly improve himself to serve as a good, well-trusted doctor.

Thomas lives by the philosophy that everyone should do something worthwhile in life.

Outside of work, Thomas spends much of his time on family, reading, nature, and volunteering. Thomas expresses that he only started actively participating in volunteer work after his Secondary years. He provided tuition to underprivileged kids

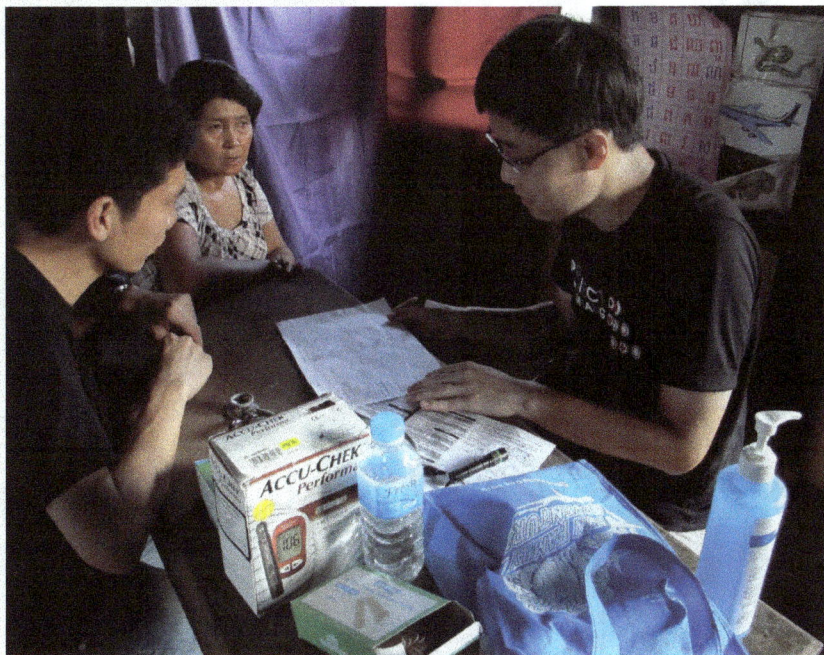

Thomas at Project Battambang 2013.

at the Bukit Ho Swee Community Service Centre (Nazareth Centre) in the 1980s and served actively as a Lector and Commentator in St. Bernadette's Church (1979–1996). He recently joined the St. Vincent De Paul Society (2014).

Thomas lives by the philosophy that everyone should do something worthwhile in life, and invest in worthy causes which interest them, without worrying too much about the rewards. The best way to succeed in life? Thomas smiles and replies that it is to follow your passion until you succeed in it.

> **Follow your passion until you succeed in it.**

For
SPORTS

For Kenneth, adventure is always calling.

Kenneth Koh

◦∿◦

Mountaineer, Class of 1981

Kenneth Koh is the first Singaporean to climb a grade VI mountaineering route (the North West Face of Half Dome in the USA in 1986). He is also a founding member and served as the first Vice-President of the Mountaineering Society of Singapore. He ran an ultramarathon in the Gobi Desert where his team finished second in 2008. The peak of these achievements was when he climbed Mt. Everest in 2011, and Aconcagua. Kenneth is a sponsored athlete for The North Face.

Did you love outdoor sports from the start?

No, actually I was a big chicken in school! I was afraid of a lot of things and maybe I still am now, but I think my love for outdoor sports grew when I was in university in the USA. Once you go overseas you have much more freedom to do whatever you want to do, and when nobody is there to make you to do stuff that makes you suffer, I learnt to grow and appreciate the outdoors. We don't have a lot of outdoors here in Singapore. We only have the nature reserves and that's the best we got, so we have to take advantage of that. I was a big chicken then, and I still

*Kenneth standing,
fifth from left.*

> **I faced many obstacles but I don't see challenges as frustrations.**

> **Get comfortable with being uncomfortable!**

am now. I don't dare to go bungee-jumping or on roller-coasters, and instead I do more stuff that I am in control of such as mountain biking and rock-climbing.

So what is the biggest obstacle or frustration you have faced?

I faced many obstacles but I don't see challenges as frustrations. Probably, the biggest challenge was my first ultramarathon. It was a desert ultramarathon, 250 km in the Gobi Desert. So I'm not really a runner; in fact I've got knee problems and I'm flat footed. So I just looked at it initially and I said this is not possible for me. But once I broke down the steps I needed to take; using the right training method, learning proper running techniques, looking into the right equipment and breaking problems into bite sized pieces, then I found it quite easy to do.

Do you have a personal philosophy or motto?

Get comfortable with being uncomfortable!

We often hear that once the physical barrier has been crossed, it is the mental state of mind that takes over. How true is this, in your opinion?

Very true. When we climbed Mount Everest, I was super tired and I was not even near the summit. I had over an hour and a half to go, and you know that climbing Everest is two things — climbing up and coming back down, and people die because they do not have the strength to come back down. So just five days before I climbed Everest, a guy died and his body was there in the mountain. He was much younger than me and his wife was giving birth to their third child while he was on expedition. This guy was highly motivated to return yet he died while returning. You have to be really motivated and trust in your training. I trusted in my training, and despite the poor weather conditions that were highly unfavourable to summit Everest, the four of us — me, my sherpa as well as two other sherpas — went ahead. I handpicked and trained with my sherpa a year before we summited.

On the descent down from Everest, I was blind. It was very windy and cold, so when I took off my goggles to de-ice them, the cold wind hit my face and froze my corneas, so I had windburn on my corneas. Because I was blind at that time we had to do a lot of complicated things — I had to put my foot on his foot as I couldn't really see where I was going. Normally, it only takes a few hours to come down. It took me eight hours to come down. But we made it.

Michael enjoys taking flight from time to time.

MICHAEL LORRAIN VAZ

---·**⚭**·---

President of Singapore Shooting Association,
President of Singapore Gun Club,
President of Asian Clay Shooting Federation,
Class of 1972

U nder Michael's leadership, the Singapore Gun Club (SGC) has become a multi-disciplined shooting club offering more than just the International Shooting Sport Federation (Olympic) clay target shooting disciplines. The SGC also offers Compak and Sporting Clay disciplines as well as International Defensive Pistol Association and Precision Pistol Competition, pistol disciplines. As the SGC Vice President in early 2000, he was the architect of the "Towkay Project" which turned the club into a profitable enterprise.

As a member of the National Shooting Team, he represented Singapore in the Commonwealth Games, World Cups and several SEA Games earning two SEA Games Bronze Medals.

Professionally, he was a fund manager. As a director of John Govett Asia in 1991, he managed a Private Equity Fund when the venture capital business was in its infancy in Singapore. He later formed his own company as an Exempt Advisor in

1999. Since 2000, he is credited with three IPO's and several trade sales of investee companies as well as the first primary listing of a US and an Australian company on the SGX. He is currently one of the founders and substantial shareholder of an Australian multi-disciplined engineering oil, gas and mining fabricator, infrastructure builder and defence contractor building warships for the Royal Australian Navy.

Michael takes aim.

"I was a national shooter for many years and still shoot competitively but I didn't want to get involved in management. In 2012, the President of SSA who was my team mate in the National Team and a friend called me and said 'I need you to take over.' I said 'No thanks.' After much persuasion I relented because I saw that shooting in Singapore was going nowhere. I said OK but I need a team to help me."

Soon, many changes were made. The Singapore Shooting Association's (SSA) policy changes saw a reduction in the large team of marginal coaches to a few world-class coaches. The SSA worked closely with the shooting clubs from schools, universities and polytechnics as partners and not adversaries or competitors. The SSA now runs four Open competitions each year to select athletes for its national training teams. Selections for the national team are strictly based on achieved scores. Coaches are now included in the SSA's panel which plans National shooting and selection programme.

"Singapore has achieved more international shooting successes in the five years since I was elected President than all the past years of shooting in Singapore. The youngest World Champion in the ISSF World Cup is a Singaporean — Martina Veloso! Singapore had never won an ISSF World Cup Medal but we now have six. Singapore had never won a quota for rifle/pistol. Two shooters won quotas and the right to shoot in the Rio Olympics. Singapore holds several current records and we now have many more shooters shooting world-class scores than ever before."

There are some in Singapore who don't think we should be placing emphasis on sports. So what would you say?

I disagree. Sport builds character and prepares one for life after sports. Sport teaches one humility and respect for others. We become aware that we cannot always be the best — there is always someone better. A sportsman must never underestimate the opponent but, instead, respect them with the view of finding a weakness to overcome them.

One must have dedication to one's sport and not fear hard work, long hours and have the determination to make great sacrifices to win. Some people don't know what it takes. They work a bit and then say it's too hard and give up.

The traits of a sportsman are the makings of a good person with the tools to succeed in the world outside sports.

66

Sport builds character and prepares one for life after sports. Sport teaches one humility and respect for others. We become aware that we cannot always be the best — there is always someone better.

99

> 66
>
> *Sportsmen make sacrifices for the glory of our nation. It is only fair that we find a way to take care of them as best as we can.*
>
> 99

You've said that it's important to ensure that athletes are well looked after they stopped competing.

Sportsmen make sacrifices for the glory of our nation. It is only fair that we find a way to take care of them as best as we can. Athletes work long hours after work or school till 9.30 pm when the Yishun Range closes. It makes for a long day. Many have to take no pay leave to compete in overseas competitions. The SSA offers them the tools to officiate at major events and get paid for their love of the sport.

The SSA hosts ISSF courses for Judges, Coaches and Referees. We encourage ex-shooters to gain the necessary licenses to officiate in ISSF competitions. Licensed officials are paid for their work and are often invited to officiate in overseas competitions.

In SSA, we prefer to employ ex-national sportsmen and will only look outside the shooting fraternity if we are unable to find ex-shooters.

NICHOLAS FANG

National Fencer and Triathlete,
Nominated Member of Parliament 2012–2015,
Class of 1991

Nicholas Fang is a well decorated sportsman who has represented Singapore in both fencing and triathlon and was National Fencing Champion (epee) for four years. He has competed in four South East Asian Games and numerous World and Asian championships. After retiring from active competition, he played a pivotal role in fencing and modern pentathlon by helming both National Sports Associations, preparing the national teams for competitions, raising funds and awareness for both sports. He served as a member of the Singapore National Olympic Council for three terms, culminating in his role as the Chef de Mission for team Singapore at the 28th SEA Games held in Singapore in 2015, securing a historic best-ever result for the host nation.

In addition to these accolades, Nicholas is a Singapore Press Holdings scholar with a Master's degree (Philosophy, Politics, Economics) from Oxford University. He worked at the Straits Times for nine years, rising to the post of Senior Correspondent. He then moved to Channel News Asia as the Business Desk Editor and news presenter.

Nicholas believes that sports training gives one a competitive edge in the corporate world.

He was most recently with Mediacorp as Deputy Chief Editor overseeing coverage of Singapore news. He is also the Executive Director of Singapore's oldest think tank, the Singapore Institute of International Affairs, and the founder and managing director of Black Dot, a multi-disciplinary strategic communications consultancy. Nicholas also served as a Nominated Member of Parliament from 2012 to 2014.

Being a former national athlete and a member of multiple sports committees in Singapore, what are your views on the traditional Asian thinking that taking on a non-office job such as sports is a foolish decision as it would not offer a stable income?

Well, that's a very common thing, it's not just an Asian thing. I think in a lot of other countries as well, there is your traditional work: a doctor, an engineer, a lawyer, a journalist. I think that, especially parents and families, they see this as something stable — you see the clear progression. Whereas when you look at sports, it is something where you have a finite lifespan: 30 plus at the most 40. After that your body does not allow you to carry on anymore at the level that you need to be at. So, your success is a little bit dependent on your talent, your skillset, and it's highly competitive because it is the world of sports. So, a lot of people will look at it and say, I can't really see the clear progression. That's I think the traditional way of looking at things. I personally think that sports has a lot of potential. If you look at the big picture, there's a lot of different parts in sports you can play. Of course, as an athlete, first and foremost but you can look at sports coaching, which is being developed into an industry in Singapore, you can move into sports administration, whether it is with Sports Singapore or with one of the National Sports Associations, or you can go into sports business. I think that there is

> **It is just a question of whether people can change their mindsets.**

❝ *When you are doing sports, you will learn a lot of core values that go into personality development. It is about teamwork, determination, discipline. It is about leadership, it's about thinking creatively, it's about understanding tactics in different sports and overcoming adversity.* **❞**

a lot of opportunity there. It is just a question of whether people can change their mindsets.

People need to understand that there is a lot of opportunity and sports can actually be seen as a huge advantage for people. It should not be seen as a disadvantage. Some say that you waste your years by becoming an athlete — those years you could have been working, in a real job and keeping up with your competitors. But, when you are doing sports, you will learn a lot of core values that go into personality development. It is about teamwork, determination, discipline. It is about leadership, it's about thinking creatively, it's about understanding tactics in different sports and overcoming adversity. More and more people are starting to realize that if you have those skills inside, it is as valuable as a piece of paper.

TEO HOCK SENG

Chairman of the Singapore Grand Prix,
Class of 1964

Teo Hock Seng helmed the world's first F1 Night Race but his first love is football. In fact, he has been heralded by many, as the "Godfather of Singapore Football". From the beginning of the new millennium up until 2015, he was the Chairman of Tampines Rovers Football Club. Under his leadership, they have been four-time S-League Champions, two-time Singapore Cup Champions and 2005 ASEAN Club Champions. In addition to his contributions on the Singapore football scene, he is the Chairman of the Singapore Grand Prix. The Singapore Grand Prix has put us on the world map as a premiere holiday destination and indeed the tourist numbers surge every September since the inaugural race in 2008.

Tell us about your classmates and teachers.

In SJI, you meet good teachers and good principals. During my 11 years in school, there was caning, which doesn't exist now. I believe caning is good for discipline, and you know, discipline was very important in my days. So, you meet all kinds of people with different thinking in SJI. As I mature, it

66
You meet all kinds of people with different thinking in SJI.
99

Teo Hock Seng represented SJI in six different sports.

is very important that the basic discipline is there, the school discipline. At assembly, we say a prayer. Before recess, we say a prayer. After recess, we say a prayer. Before we leave school, we say a prayer. Four times a day. Not many schools had that.

Are you a Catholic?

I am not a Catholic. It is not necessary to be a Catholic, but this discipline is embedded in you for life. As for teachers, many teachers were strict, many teachers were good, and many teachers were helpful. At my time in SJI, there were two brothers who are no longer around — Brother Hyacinth and Brother Sylvester.

What's your best memory of SJI?

My best memory in SJI? I represented the school in six sports. For rugby, I got school colours. I played a lot of rugby for the school. And I'm still supporting rugby today *(points at HSBC Singapore Rugby Sevens 2016 event card)*. Study wise, in academics, I did well enough to pass. Good enough to go to university, good enough to get a good job.

I think today, you have to be more pragmatic in life. You have to be more open-hearted, you have to be more charitable, if you can afford to. If you can't, then you should do some volunteer work, which does help to develop the character of students.

So have you been involved in volunteer work before?

Yes, yes. I am the chairman of the Singapore GP. It's a volunteer job, I get no reward for doing this. Just the satisfaction of a job well done.

> **You have to be more open-hearted, you have to be more charitable, if you can afford to. If you can't, then you should do some volunteer work.**

So where do you get inspiration for this?

Well, it's a group of friends who gave me this challenge. They asked me to chair the Board of Directors, so I said okay. Of course, it is not easy. Like football, they asked me to be the chairman of Tampines Rovers. Of course, last time in the league, there were 11 teams. Tampines Rovers was always 9, 10, 11, the last three. Now, they are a championship team.

I think the spirit is to challenge yourself to win — in sports, in work. Sports-minded people work harder, I think so.

You employ former footballers from Tampines Rovers here? Why do you do that?

I prefer employing sportsmen than non-sportsmen, everything being equal. I think sportsmen have a bit more flair, they are a little bit more enterprising. These people are like House Captains, where you must be good at sports, and you are elected by the school community, and thus it is a big responsibility. When they play for you, they play 100%.

Those people working for you here, do you believe in giving them the opportunity to excel?

Of course! In my car rental division, I have Yunos Samad who used to play football for me in 2002. Back then, he was working as a clerk. Now, he can handle my entire car rental division, as a manager. He understands what to do, he has potential, and he works hard.

66

I prefer employing sportsmen than non-sportsmen, everything being equal. I think sportsmen have a bit more flair, they are a little bit more enterprising.

99

How do you encourage more young people in Singapore to engage in volunteer work?

It's very hard. There's a lot of help needed in the community and people don't realise until they are involved. Volunteering has no age limit. Young people should get involved, you all should try to get involved.

The spirit of wanting to help must be embedded in you first. If you are given the power, or you have leadership qualities, then you are able to organise activities.

> *Volunteering has no age limit. Young people should get involved, you all should try to get involved.*

For the
ECONOMY

Mr Tie receiving the Community Chest Special Contribution award from the former President, Dr Tony Tan.

EDMUND TIE

Chairman & Founder of Edmund Tie & Company,
Class of 1963/65

E dmund Tie has over 40 years of experience in real estate consultancy and is widely regarded as one of Asia's leading property consultants. Formerly the Managing Director of a leading international property consultancy in Singapore, Edmund established Edmund Tie & Company in 1995 together with 12 founding partners, breaking new ground in the real estate advisory business in Southeast Asia. Edmund is well sought after by governments and academia who are very keen to tap on his expertise. He has shared the wealth of his experience with the National University of Singapore, the Real Estate Developer's Association, the Urban Redevelopment Authority and the Ministry of National Development.

Edmund is also well known for his extensive social and community service. Over the years, he has led many major charity drives and helped raise funds exceeding $12 million, mainly for the Community Chest. In recognition of this work, he was awarded the Public Service Medal (PBM) at the National Day Awards 2001 and subsequently the *Bintang Bakti Masyarakat (BBM)*[1] in 2006. He

---

[1] Public Service Star.

was also conferred the Community Chest Special Recognition Award in 2014. Edmund, who has been active in the local arts scene as well, has received the Arts Supporter Award 2003 from the National Arts Council.

What do you remember about your time at SJI?

I was part of the first cohort in St. Michael's School which is now St. Joseph's Institution Junior. I think it was 1952 when I was five or six. Just before the Primary 6 exams, because my family and my friends came from Sarawak in East Malaysia, they wanted to emigrate back. So I was transferred to St. Joseph's School in Kuching in East Malaysia where I sat for my Primary 6 exam. Because I did so well, they gave me a double promotion to Form 2 so I skipped Form 1. Then I returned to SJI in Singapore to complete my O-Levels and A-Levels and graduated in 1965. During my time in SJI, I was a school prefect and was also president of the St. Vincent de Paul (SVDP) Society.

66

We passed the hat around to take up a collection every month amongst the students in each class to help support their fellow students who came from disadvantaged or poor families.

99

We had to appoint one class representative for the SVDP each year and we passed the hat around to take up a collection every month amongst the students in each class to help support their fellow students who came from disadvantaged or poor families. Occasionally we took the funds, accounted for the money and made distributions during our visits to the students' homes to see how they are doing, how they are progressing, how their family is coping — so that's how I started helping the school as well. I could see the realities of kids who were so poor, who came to school with torn shoes and in tattered uniforms, and without having their meals. People coming from poor living backgrounds, so that was basically an eye opener for me.

One of my best memories was being in the LDDS. I was a member of the play "Arsenic and Old

Lace" at the Victoria Theatre. What happened on Opening Night was very significant — there was a racial riot! If I finished A-level in '65 it should be in '64. So the police came and told us all to cancel the play halfway through and brought us back home because of the riots. So it was something quite significant in Singapore's political history.

What are your memories of establishing your first company?

It was very daunting, because I think I worked for almost 20 years, trying to build up a company from scratch and my departure was very widely publicised. The daunting challenge was starting from scratch with nothing but people because it was a people business. But interestingly, at the launch of my company I had a special inauguration. I invited the late President Wee Kim Wee to be my guest of honour where I sponsored an art exhibition of Singapore's well known artists to raise funds for charity and to promote my company. It was a three-pronged strategy, promote local artists, raise funds for The Rainbow Centre and launch the company. You know The Rainbow Centre? It is a centre for children suffering from multiple disabilities located at Margaret Drive Special School. So I killed three birds with one stone. I had an exhibition and the company was launched in the Marriott hotel ballroom. And in the invitation to all my guests I wrote "If you are considering sending congratulatory flowers, press messages or gifts, may we invite you to share our concern for the less privileged by donating to Margaret Drive Special School instead?" They all did this and on the day of the inauguration, you could see that the walkway from the lifts all the way to the ballroom were lined with floral bouquets. So not only did they make a donation but they also sent us floral bouquets which was very, very touching. If you go

> *It was a three-pronged strategy, promote local artists, raise funds for The Rainbow Centre and launch the company.*

to The Rainbow Centre today you will see several facilities named after Edmund Tie & Company. These were donated over 20 years ago.

What's the best way to get more people to be kind?

I think just by example, and by being an instrument of His peace — to motivate other people by sharing your views, your aspirations towards helping the poor, the sick and the unfortunate. I'm not sharing this with you to beat my chest or boast about my achievements, but I just want to lay it out for you, so that you can get an idea as to what I'm talking about. I think by what I do publicly in terms of fundraising and my charity galas, hopefully I'm building up a greater awareness of the plight of the disadvantaged. I use the advantage that I have in my network of communications especially in the corporate sector, to get companies who are better equipped financially to help society as a whole.

What advice do you have for young people today?

Always strive to maintain the highest standards of professionalism, integrity and trust. When I started, as a Trainee Valuer I was paid an allowance of $75 a month, and I never asked for any increment. After three months, when my boss saw how hardworking I was, my allowance was increased to $150. In another three months, to $200. In another three months, to $250. So I never asked for any increment. I just worked, always willing and ready to be humble and diligent in taking on assignments to broaden my experience and exposure to build a successful career. Because it's not just paper qualifications. You have to build up your experience, reputation, expertise and client goodwill. The lesson is always to strive to maintain the highest standards of professionalism, integrity and trust in doing business. These are very important attributes.

> 66
> *I think by what I do publicly in terms of fundraising and my charity galas, hopefully I'm building up a greater awareness of the plight of the disadvantaged.*
> 99

ESMOND CHOO

Senior Executive Director, UOB Kay Hian,
Class of 1975

E smond Choo attended St. Michael's School from 1964 to 1969. He then studied at SJI from 1970 to 1975 and was part of the last graduating class of A-level students from SJI before the formation of Catholic Junior College in 1975. Amongst his various CCA activities, he was a scout leader with the 2104 Pelandok Scout Group between 1974 to 1975. He graduated with honours in Commerce from Melbourne University (Australia) in 1981 and qualified as a Chartered Accountant with the Australian Institute of Chartered Accountants in 1986. He was lauded with academic accolades such as the Melbourne University exhibition prizes for corporate law (1979) and taxation law (1981). He has accumulated substantial experience in the finance and insurance sectors since 1986. He is the former Chairman of the Stockbrokers' Association of Singapore and sits on various industry Committees including the recent MAS Financial Advisory Industry Review Committee. He is also active in community service and development.

> *I think my time spent with the 2104 Venture Scout troop engendered in me a strong pioneering spirit.*

"I think my time spent with the 2104 Venture Scout troop engendered in me a strong pioneering

Esmond feels that the strong Lasallian education inspired in him an instinctive love for God.

spirit. Every weekend, we could be hiking at night deep in the catchment areas in Singapore or the rural farmlands in Pulau Ubin by day. That gave us a great sense of adventure and independence!"

"One of the highlights then was when we competed and won a $2,000 government grant for an expedition by 20 scouts; the youngest was only 14 years of age and I was the oldest, barely 17."

"Our winning proposal was to travel to Penang from Singapore commuting by different modes of transportation — public bus, rail, ferry and eventually returning home by air. Over a two-week period, the route took us from Victoria Street to Johor Bahru, then to Malacca, Port Dickson, Cameron Highlands, Ipoh, Penang, Kuala Lumpur and from Kuala Lumpur by air to Singapore. We planned the entire trip on our own without any help from our teachers. Back in 1974, $2,000 was a huge sum but what we managed to get out of the trip was a priceless experience."

"Our journey exposed us to a myriad of experiences. Some were pretty rough but with God's grace we all returned intact richer with the experience. Our patron St. Joseph must have worked round the clock to ensure our safety!"

"We stayed in cheap guest houses and budget accommodation. It was amazing how we did it because there were no trip advisors. I remember when we were in Penang sitting in a coffee shop and it was really hot and sultry! I had a splitting headache and took out a Panadol tablet and swallowed it. Back in the 70s, Penang was a haven for sex and drugs. A guy came up to me and asked me if it was an MX pill (a popular narcotic drug then) and whether I had a cheap source! If you did not have a strong moral compass on you, you could easily have been influenced by the things which went on then. It was just amazing how we got by."

"We spent our $2,000 on all kinds of things — food, accommodation, passage, the odd rum and coke, the lot! Much were in small establishments which did not have a habit of issuing receipts."

"At that time, the late Brother Patrick was the principal. He asked me 'How was the trip?' I said it was very good. 'By the way could you write me a

> 66
> *Our journey exposed us to a myriad of experiences. Some were pretty rough but with God's grace we all returned intact richer with the experience. Our patron St. Joseph must have worked round the clock to ensure our safety!*
> 99

statement on how you spent your $2,000 backed by receipts?'"

"I felt rather sick in the stomach as no one told me before we left for the trip that I had to do a financial statement, let alone produce receipts! All I had was a log of our trip experiences. I only had receipts for airline, train, ferry tickets and one hotel. There were no credit card statements to fall back on in those days! It was again through divine intervention that I was able to reconstruct the accounts for every dollar spent complete with required payment vouchers — my baby steps towards a career in chartered accountancy and investment banking! The government was happy enough not to want to take back the pile of cash they gave us! Those were some of the wonderful individual experiences that made me a Josephian."

"The rich individual experience coupled with the strong Lasallian education received at SJI indelibly etched in my soul and consciousness the instinctive love for God, the respect and empathy for humanity, and the discipline and fortitude to see to completion the tasks I set out to do."

"My education in SJI guided me to deal wisely and fairly with the many issues and challenges faced in living out my leadership responsibilities and everyday life — always sparing a thought for the last, the lost and the least that are less fortunate than us."

66

My education in SJI guided me to deal wisely and fairly with the many issues and challenges faced in living out my leadership responsibilities.

99

MANU BHASKARAN

Director of Centennial Group;
Chief Executive, Centennial Asia Advisors,
Class of 1974

Manu Bhaskaran is Director of Centennial Group International and the Founding Director and Chief Executive Officer of Centennial Asia Advisors. Manu has more than 30 years of expertise in economic and political risk assessment and forecasting in Asia. Before joining the Centennial Group, he was Chief Economist for Asia of Société Générale Investment Bank, Asia and managed its Singapore-based economic advisory group. Manu is a well-regarded commentator on Asian financial and economic affairs, and has regular columns in business weeklies such as *The Edge* in Singapore and Malaysia. He serves as Member of the Regional Advisory Board for Asia of the International Monetary Fund; Senior Adjunct Fellow, Institute of Policy Studies; Council Member of the Singapore Institute of International Affairs; and Vice-President of the Economics Society of Singapore. Manu has a Master's degree in Public Administration from the John F. Kennedy School of Government at Harvard University and a Bachelor's degree in economics from Cambridge University. He has also qualified as a Chartered Financial Analyst. He is also an Adjunct

For Manu, SJI friends are the friends that stay with you for life.

Senior Research Fellow at the Institute of Policy Studies, Singapore.

"I spent four years in SJI, because I was in the first batch of Catholic Junior College so I didn't do Pre-U. So I had four years there and definitely very treasured memories of those four years because those are your growing up years. First of all it's your teachers. I am very happy to say that every year I had very good teachers, very inspiring teachers. Every subject had really, really good teachers who took an interest in me, who encouraged me. I have very fond memories of them, especially my form teacher in Sec 4 Mr Dominic Yip, who was the principal of St. Michael's, I think he still helps out, and my Malay teacher, Che Zarazillah — I think he was the best second language teacher I ever had, he really made second language interesting."

"Second of course are the friends you make. The friends that you make at this age are the friends that will stay with you for life — that I think is very important. The third thing is that, when I look back, you know the difference that SJI made is that it does emphasise more on values — that is very important these days, and is something we can easily forget but a school that is built on those foundations, a mission school, will carry these ideas. I am not saying that non-mission schools don't teach morals, because they do. But here is the passionate conviction of the people and the people who manage it, the brothers, guide its strategy and so on. That is still very, very important to me, which is why I insisted my son go to SJI International."

When asked about his involvement in co-curricular activities, he reveals that his business acumen, ingenuity and capacity for hard work may have demonstrated itself during his time at SJI.

> *The difference that SJI made is that it does emphasise more on values — that is very important these days, and is something we can easily forget but a school that is built on those foundations, a mission school, will carry these ideas.*

> *His business acumen, ingenuity and capacity for hard work may have demonstrated itself during his time at SJI.*

"I was a debater. I was not much of a sportsman, so the sports I did was just cross-country running. I was in the debate team, and I think I was the vice president or treasurer of the stamps club. We had a Stamp Club where we used to actually make quite a lot of money because a lot of teachers were collectors of the first day covers. We knew when first day of covers were issued — we queued up on Sunday morning outside the General Post Office, which is now the Fullerton Hotel and bought a lot of the first day covers and charged the service charge for it. We made money for the club that way."

PETER SEAH

Chairman, DBS Group Holdings and Singapore Airlines, Class of 1962

Peter Seah joined the Board of Directors of DBS Group Holdings Ltd and DBS Bank Ltd on 16 November 2009 and assumed the role of Chairman on 1 May 2010. In addition, he is Chairman of DBS Bank (Hong Kong) Ltd. He was appointed Chairman of Singapore Airlines on 1 January 2017. Peter is the present Chairman of Singapore Health Services Pte Ltd and LaSalle College of the Arts Ltd. Peter was a banker for 33 years before retiring as Vice Chairman and CEO of the former Overseas Union Bank in 2001. Peter serves on the boards of GIC Pte Ltd, Fullerton Financial Holdings Pte Ltd and STT Communications Ltd. He is also Chairman of the National Wages Council and a member of the Presidential Elections Committee.

Peter was awarded the Distinguished Service Order by the President of Singapore in 2012.

SJI provided a moral compass for Peter.

What was your CCA in SJI?

No CCA, play truant! I was just your regular student playing games like table tennis. What I was most active in wasn't part of the school but I joined St. John's Ambulance Brigade (SJAB) outside of school, which was my own chosen CCA. In my time, we didn't get points for CCA. You just did things you had an interest in because you wanted to do it — because it's something you enjoy doing. I suppose I found interest in SJAB. When you are part of St John's Ambulance Brigade, you get to participate in a lot of activities. You are taught first aid, home nursing and foot drill. You get to do duties outside school. You get to go to the turf club and sit in the jeep that follows the horses as they race just in case somebody gets hurt. Basically I found it interesting because it prepared you to be able to help people who are injured. You learn everything — in home nursing you learn to give injections and other skills that nurses are taught. You learn things that are not part of your curriculum, not in your textbooks.

What are your best memories of being at SJI?

SJI holds a lot of fond memories for me because many of my friends till today were my classmates. We finished our A-Levels together, we went to university together and we still meet regularly for lunch after 50 years. The memories of comradeship and friendship are not just from studying but from having fun together and growing up together. We also have fond memories of my old school teachers. Part and parcel of growing up is when we run foul of school regulations and get punished. I think students should not only remember the times when they did good but also remember the times when they got in trouble. That is when they learn life lessons and about the things you should not do. Being naughty is part of preparing you for life. The overall development of an individual does not come from just studying. SJI helps students by giving them a lot of moral values. Catholic values are very strong moral values. They help provide a moral compass which pretty much guides our values. Many of my classmates including those who are not Catholics have these shared values.

> **"**
> *I found it interesting because it prepared you to be able to help people who are injured. You learn everything — in home nursing you learn to give injections and other skills that nurses are taught. You learn things that are not part of your curriculum, not in your textbooks.*
> **"**

The La Salle Brothers were role models for Philip.

Philip Seah

CEO, Prudential Assurance Company Singapore,
Class of 1971

Philip Seah assumed the position of CEO of Prudential Assurance Company Singapore (Prudential Singapore) from 22 October 2015, for a second time. He was their CEO from 2006 to 2010. He first joined Prudential Singapore as a part time life insurance agent in 1978 while working as a flight steward with Singapore Airlines. He became a full-time life insurance agent in 1979 and progressed rapidly through the ranks to become a senior agency manager. In the process, he was involved in the Life Underwriters Association and rose to become its President in 1989. His passion, commitment and achievements were noticed by Prudential Singapore's senior management and this led to his appointment as Assistant General Manager in 1990. After many other roles in Singapore as well as Hong Kong and Philippines, he was promoted to CEO in 2006.

"I was from a government school. My father was a Josephian and it was he who led me to SJI. On the first day at SJI in 1968, I didn't know anyone at all. I was petrified! All the other students seemed to know each other having come from the feeder schools. I also observed they were all wearing the school tie and I wasn't. I didn't even know how to put on a tie. I was very alone and did not feel like I belonged. So I bought the school tie and spent the night practicing to knot the tie. The next day I went to school proudly wearing the tie. Of course I was the only boy wearing a tie then! As I stood there feeling confused and silly, one of my classmates realised my predicament and explained the dress code. I have always remembered him for that act of kindness."

"I was involved in debates and public speaking from Secondary 1. Our teacher Mr G. V. Santho insisted that we not read from our notes and use body language to emphasise our points. I'm very grateful to Mr Santho for teaching this invaluable life skill because I have come to fully realise how important it is in life to be able to present my thoughts clearly and eloquently."

> **When I think about being 'a man for others', the best examples are the La Salle Brothers — how they have devoted their lives to the students. This is imbued in many SJI boys. Nobody taught that in class — it was taught through role modeling.**

"When I think about being 'a man for others', the best examples are the La Salle Brothers — how they have devoted their lives to the students. This is imbued in many SJI boys. Nobody taught that in class — it was taught through role modeling. Some of my cohort such as Michael Broughton, inspired by that dedication, went back to SJI to extend that legacy. He became a La Salle Brother, taught in SJI and rose to become the Vice Principal. His love for SJI brought him back to serve."

"Some schools boast of producing captains of industries. Other schools produce many senior government officials. I am very proud that SJI produces boys who serve, all over, deeply imbued by the ethos of being — A Man for Others."

Acknowledgements

With thanks to:

The 10th SJI Board of Governors for commissioning this book.

The *For Others* Committee for assisting in selecting the interviewees —
Mr Anthony Lim, Dr Bernard Thio, Mr Derek Loh, Mr Jeffrey Low,
Prof Leo Tan, Mr Mark Wong, Prof Michael Chia, Mr Roy Quek,
Mr Tan Teck Hock, and Mr Theodore Chan.

Professor Tan Cheng Han for writing the Foreword.

Fr. Adrian Danker, Principal of SJI
for giving his full support to this project.

SJI English teachers — Mrs Sandra Lee, Mrs Beryl Ang,
Mrs Elizabeth Scott and Ms Sophie Heike, and all their students
who helped with the interviews and profiles.

Ms Eliza Lim for her administrative assistance.

Mr Jiang Yulin from World Scientific who provided his editorial
support for this project.

Teachers in Charge of Students Interviewers
Mrs Beryl Ang, Mrs Elizabeth Scott and Ms Sophie Heike

Student Editors
Mr Thaddeus Han Wen Jiang (IB Class of 2017)
Ms Teoh Le Yi (IB Class of 2017)

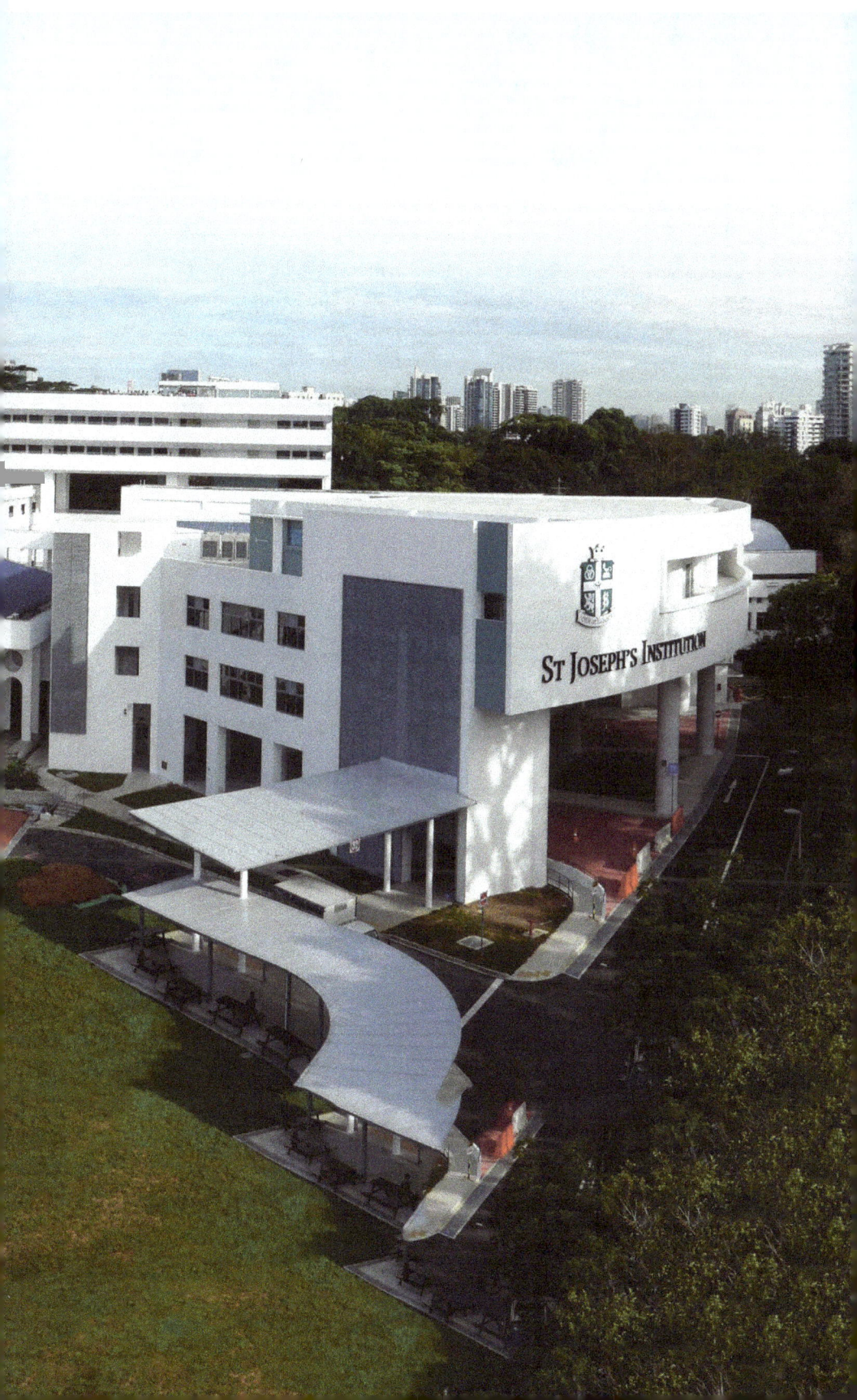

Student Interviewers from the Class of 2016

Fintan 402

Adithya Suresh
Adriel Triston Ong Jun
Anand Chaanan Singh
Ang Le Wayne
Aw Kinn
Chin Si Yuan, Nigel
Darryll Edmund
Dylan Christian Tang Jun Wen
Foo Zheng Lin, Marcus
Geraldo Nick K Kanayalal
Haris B Dzulkifli
Ivan Neo
Joel Luke Tan Yi
John Paul Lim Jie Min

Jonathan Audie Widjaja
Joshua Lim Shouyan
Justin Alfonso S Pansacola
K Naveen Lakshmanan
Kaemon Ng Chongyu
Matthew Liu Zhen Jie
Mohamed Taufiq B Mohamed H
R Rethik Raj
Ryan Koh Rei En
Samuel Murugasu
Shaun Hue Yong Shan
Tristan Maximilian Smith
Zikry Nasrullah B Zairul Azidin

Lawrence 402

Adam Norman Barrell
Adriel Ng Jing Da
Aidan James Cheah
Aung Khant Soe
Brandon Lau Ming Jun
Brendan Teo Tze Ern
Francis Ethan Wee Shen Liang
Gao Xiaoyuan
Hud B Mohammed Helmi
Jay Parmar
Jonathan Ramakrishna
Jordan Joseph Stanley
Lee Chuan Cheng
Lee Rui Zhe
Lee Yhu Fhei
Lee Zhexian Thaddeus
Liew Kai Wei

Marcus James Phua Zhen Rong
Ng Chee Kiat, Jerome
Ng Sheng Yuan
Ng Yue Han, Jared
Ong Jun Xun
Ryan Woon Kai Jie
Sean Teo Pang Boon
Snodgrass Andrew Mark
Sreenivasan Bindhu Nikhil V
Suriyaprakash
Tan Hsien Jie, Jared
Tan Jin Wei Daniel
Tan Ying-Shuen Nicholas
Toh Kevan
Tyrone Santiago
Yogesh Adhi Narayan
Yuknavell S/O Thiyagarajan

Marcian 403

Arunkumar Praveen
Bryan Yeo
Chia Jeng Yee
Denzil John Gomes
Emmanuel Jason Adrianus Sutanto
Eu Chun Yong
Ezekiel Ang Zi Wei
Gabriel Soh Yong Kiat
Jed Lim Shouheng
Jerrie B Zainul Shaffee
L Shasshen
Lim Yan Xun Luke
Matthew Gan Ziqin

Ng Sze Yeow
Prateesh Pillai Sanjeevi Saravanan
Sar Jun Wei
Senthil Kumar Dhanabalan
Shiva Bharathi Gupta
Su Liheng, Benjamin
Tay Xi-Rui Benjamin John
Teo Hock Hon Bernard
Thomas De Silva
Wells Chin Shijian
Zachary Caius Lim Tze Yan
Zaki B Zainudin

Michael 401

Aaron Li Wen Hao
Andrew Seah Wai Kit
Arthur Kaki Fong Zhi Ming
Brian Lim Kaishun
Chang Yu Ern, Matthew
Chew Ann Kim
David Gareth Ong
Ho Zi Jian Pierre
Isaac Yap Yi Yu
Jansen Ryan Patrick
Jeremy Stephen Silva
Joel Koh Yu Han
Jonathan Lee Zi Han
Kevin Lim Jia Le
Lai Kit

Lim Peng Yong Darren
Mohamed Czarmir Ikraam S/O M A
Nam Harin
Ow Jun Hao, John
Pereira Brandon Scott
Ray Yeo
Samuel Tay Zi Bin
Shane Alexander Keiser
Shaun Tan Yong Han
Tan Wei Fan
Teo Yu Xiang Wesley
Timotius Matthew Avandyasvara
Tommy Samuel Tsang Hing Lam
Tristan Tan Tng En
Zachary Yee Zhuo Zeng

Student Interviewers from the Class of 2016

*Michael 404*_____

Andre Lim Yu Xuan

Chen De Han Brendan

Chong Qi Rong

Christopher Thian Wen Long

Daniel Suresh Thomas

Foo Wen Jie Jerald

Ham Wee Jian James

Hari Menon

Jeff Thng Wen Han

John Christopher Phang Yong W

Justin Tan

Kwan Zhi Xuan Jacob

Loke E-Hao, Brendan

Muhammad Zulkhairi B Hamdan

Neil Bhargava

Nicholas Pua Hsien Han

Rodrigues Andre John

Ryan Tok Wie Chen

Scott Ngai Tze Hei

Sharan Vaitheswaran

Toh Pei Qi

Vikraman Venketasubramanian

Yong Chong Huan

www.ingramcontent.com/pod-product-compliance
Lightning Source LLC
Chambersburg PA
CBHW052005270326
41929CB00015B/2800